D0471266

Travis

Enjoy and
play well

Best

Joe B____
8/31/17

JOSEPH BRONSON

GOLF
CHRONICLES

An Amateur's Lifelong Dedication to the Game

outskirtspress
DENVER, COLORADO

Outskirts Press, Inc.
http://www.outskirtspress.com

ISBN: 978-1-4787-7279-8

Outskirts Press and the "OP" logo are trademarks belonging to Outskirts Press, Inc.

PRINTED IN THE UNITED STATES OF AMERICA

Dedicated to:

Amateurs: Frank Nunley, Jeet Harika, Bill Husak,
Barry Hartwyk, Walt Hussey, and Tom Rohrs

Teaching Professional: Ray Otis, Jr.

Caddie: Richard Torrez

PREFACE

Golf Chronicles is about experiences with golf from a number of different perspectives. I wanted to challenge myself to write a book that is differentiated from most, if not all, golf books. The book looks at golf from a number of different angles, from my personal experiences to essays and commentary about the current state of the game. Golf is a microcosm of life and the book is sprinkled with some philosophy on the nuances of the game. It's not just a story about myself, but I have attempted to tell a story about golf through the lens of a participant who loves the game.

I've had a number of experiences in playing courses and areas of the world that many people have played and can relate to. However, I believe very few people have had the combined experience that I've had in playing golf all over the United States and the world. I've played 85 courses in the top 100 in the United States. I've played all of the British Open venues past and present at least once, and some of them many times. I've played in Ireland, Italy, France, Portugal, and Spain in Europe; and China, Japan, Singapore, Malaysia, Australia, New Zealand, and even Israel. Israel has only one golf course in the entire country. I've tried to illustrate these experiences and observe, sometimes with a skeptical eye, the subtleties of the different venues.

The book is organized as a series of chronicles of life stories and vignettes of playing golf, philosophies of the game itself, and some experiences that I consider to be unique. Every golfer has their own unique experience and, in this work, I've assembled a wide variety of topics to give the reader a sense of how great the game is.

I decided to treat *Chronicles* randomly so the book is not sequenced in time. It is designed to change topics and subjects quickly, from autobiographical tales to philosophies about the game and experiences. *Chronicles* should be viewed as a series of essays about the game of golf, as observed by a very ordinary player who loves the game. There is no discussion of winning club championships, hobnobbing with PGA professionals, or suggestions on how to improve anyone's game. Golf is and has been a major part of my life, and I hope it will enrich the experience of anyone who plays the game, and those individuals who don't play at all.

I've dedicated this book to my wife Linda, the love of my life, and my best friend and mentor, Brian Shirley, my son Ian, and my daughter Meredith.

Linda doesn't play golf. She has been supportive all the time we've spent together raising children while I worked; she has supported my golf habit and has been the beneficiary of my happiness after a good round of golf. Linda is heavily into jewelry. She has a collection of very expensive things acquired over the years and some of them have occurred in my euphoria after having broken 80 at some resort or venue on vacation. She has enough jewelry to start her own store, but she would rather continue to acquire these things. Some of her pieces have been displayed in art galleries throughout the United States.

Linda's experiences on the golf course have been few but memorable. She once took up the game before we had kids, taking some lessons near our home in Fairfield, Connecticut. I didn't believe that she would stick with it, so I bought her only a 7 iron. I was correct, as the difficulty of the game and the time required simply bored her. The lessons vaporized and that was the end of her career. I had the audacity to have her ride on a golf cart with me on the Williams College Golf Course when she was seven months pregnant with our son Ian. This wasn't a particularly good idea since Ian was born a month later prematurely on November 1. She had a blast attending the Masters with me as well as the Ryder Cup in her hometown of Rochester, New York at Oakhill Country Club. She used to watch me play in the pro-ams, but couldn't look for fear that I would hit a bad shot into the crowd (which I never did). So Linda's connection with golf is distant and would be nonexistent if it weren't for me. I have given Linda the handle of "AWOT"—which stands for "Athletic Waste of Time." Most women would revile such a term, but Linda actually embraces it. She is a wonderful lady.

Linda has taken care of the family and me for the past forty-three years and continues to support me in golf and every endeavor that I am involved in over the years. She has always been encouraging with me about my game and that is the little "extra" I carry around with me at every round.

My son Ian has been playing golf since he was six years old. He began his golf career by taking lessons from a professional at the local driving range for an hour a week. By the age of eight, he was playing the golf course from the women's tees and has a terrific swing and overall mechanics. When we moved to England in 1991, he was able to play golf at St. Andrews, Gleneagles, and other venues throughout the country. He's played in Japan, Ireland, and Portugal. At age sixteen, he was very interested in getting his first car--a black Ford Mustang. I told him we would play for the car on the golf course in match play. After 18 holes, the match was halved and we decided to settle the matter on the practice putting green. He won the playoff and I presented him with a toy model of the Ford Mustang. We did play for a car, but we didn't specify what kind of car. He eventually got the car anyway. Golf has been a lifelong competitive activity for the two of us and we've played together all over the world. We've discussed everything on the course, from teachers, sports, the facts of life, girlfriends, professors, bosses, careers, and everything in between. What I like best about playing golf with your son is that you always win—you win when you beat him and you win when you lose to him, as he goes home to brag to his mother. We're still playing together, but now that he's married, our outings are Father's Day, my birthday, and holidays. He amazes me with his good play despite the limited amount of times he plays now. He usually beats me like a drum.

Brian Shirley is my golfing mentor. He is responsible for whatever prosperity I have achieved in my golf game. He is also one of the few people I can count (outside of my family) as a true friend. We've been able to maintain a close relationship for the last forty years despite living 5,000 miles away from each other. From 1990-1995 we lived in England so we were very close during that period and enjoyed many social engagements together with our family. We have been playing together for the past forty years. Our meeting was founded on a boss/subordinate relationship. I was the global director of accounting for Fairchild Camera and Instrument Corporation with overall corporate responsibility, and Brian was the controller of the European organization based in London. During the acquisition of Fairchild by Schlumberger, Ltd., Fairchild European headquarters moved to Paris and Brian commuted back and forth to his home in London to manage the financial aspects of the transition.

I can't remember why, but we became fast friends with a common interest in golf, except for one significant difference. In 1979 Brian was (and still is) a player of immense skill, and in 1979 I was an unskilled hacker.

Brian and I started playing together when he visited the US for work. As boss and subordinate we got along well and shared ideas about our business. I was chartered with completing the integration of Fairchild into Schlumberger and also integration of the Fairchild business units into Schlumberger's business processes. Brian never coached me about my terrible technique, grip, stance etc. In those years I struggled with the driver, but seemed always to be able to hit iron shots relatively well and formed the basic strength for my game for years. He always beat me, but he was the far superior player and I yearned to be competitive. Brian has the short game of a professional and I always tell him that anything within 50 yards is "Shirley Land," meaning that he usually always gets up and down. Thanks to his help, we are able to play each other today straight up, and I would have never made progress without his skill and coaching.

A few years later Brian was transferred to another unit of Schlumberger and I eventually left Fairchild/Schlumberger in 1984 for the greener pastures of Applied Materials, Inc. Our communications were sporadic and we didn't play much golf together for the next five years, but nevertheless we stayed in touch with each other. Of course, I lied about the progress I was making in my golf game.

In 1990 I was offered the opportunity to become a general manager in the company, but I had to move to England to run a very troubled operation. I was able to now see Brian and his family frequently and we started playing golf together virtually every weekend. Brian lived in Ealing, a very lovely part of West London, and had his office in downtown London right next to Harrods.

He was a member of Richmond Golf Club for many years and his brother Roy and I played many a round at the Richmond Golf Club.

Brian has the golf swing of the gods. Every time I took him to our club in California, our playing partners would always comment on the grace and purity of his golf swing. It is perfect and remains so at age seventy-two. He also has the short game of a professional and is responsible for my short game, which I would label "pretty good," but not in his league. When we play together and he misses a green with his approach shot—if the shot is within 30 yards of the hole—it is almost always a par. I would guess that his "up and down" ratio is over 80%. A professional would love to have his short game.

Whenever Brian and I played with my friends or members of my golf club in the United States, he was always complemented for his swing and technique. It would happen even if we played with strangers paired up playing on the Monterrey Peninsula.

Brian grew up playing golf in Troon, Scotland and reminisces fondly about his days as a lad who would just go out with his friends after school on the golf course and just play until dark.

My daughter Meredith also doesn't play golf. She has taken a battery of lessons and is a natural athlete. As a child, she was good at so many sports that we told her she had to focus on one sport. She chose swimming and has had a distinguished career in high school and post school. She is a tremendous competitor and has an uncanny way of focusing on her technique and how it impacts her performance. She is still swimming today in Masters competitions and has medaled consistently in US National events. She overcame many obstacles to reach her goal to become an attorney, and now practices law at a major corporation. She is an inspiration to me, but the new Titleist woods and irons continue to collect dust in her closet. Maybe someday....

TABLE OF CONTENTS

Chapter 1
GOLF

What is it about golf? What is this ridiculous game where people hit a small tiny ball with a stick around six miles of ground? People who don't play golf often wonder why so many people play so frequently and why it is so enjoyable to them. Golf is more than a game. It's a reflection of who we are as human beings, how we interact with each other, and a measure of character. Golf is also a reflection of life and the ups and downs of the breaks, opportunities, and bad luck. A well-struck tee shot at the ninth hole at Cordevalle in San Martin, California will most of the time invariably end up in the ditch that cuts the center of the fairway just like a knife. The same shot on virtually any other golf hole will produce a short iron to the green. Golf, like life, is a big challenge where all the practice in the world is not necessarily a key to success--but without it, you simply cannot excel.

Golf is hard. A very successful technologist and product innovator decided to take up the game in his late forties. He had done so well at product innovation that he was able to take these skills into managing a business. For skills he did not possess, he read management books voraciously and believed that anything could be picked up and learned. He learned scuba diving, photography and various other interests. When he utilized this technique to the game of golf he came up empty…he couldn't understand why he couldn't hit the golf ball and just pick it up. He became frustrated and quickly discarded the game, failing to understand its true meaning. Golf is a challenge and the golf course is a good place to check your ego as you pull into the parking lot. No matter how good you think you are, there are literally thousands of people who are better than you. The life of professional golf and the upper echelons of the world of amateur golf are also great examples, as many who have starred in the game are unable to sustain their power.… witness the likes of David Duval, Ian Baker Finch, and countless others who won major championships but could not sustain their performance.

The game of golf is a challenge, but can be the most pleasant form of relaxation. It is a game you play against yourself. You are consistently battling your brain, debating whether you can hit this shot or not. It does not matter of the level of skill involved, whether it's Tiger Woods hitting the ball out of 8" of rough in the British Open, or Joe Bronson hitting a seven wood over trees fifty yards away on the 17th hole at Almaden Country Club. The question always remains: "Do you have the skill to execute the shot without failing?"

The game requires that you have confidence in yourself to be able to master shots and techniques that you want to succeed at. Jack Nicklaus was a master of focus and visualization, sizing up his shot and taking dead aim at his target. We've seen golfers who curse and berate themselves for every shot that comes up short of their expectations. While this emotion might seem reasonable to most of us, sometimes it occurs on every shot hit—even the good ones. In golf, the glass is either half empty or half full. It's a lot more practical to take the half full approach. The game is too difficult. You have to remember the good shots and toss away the bad ones as exceptions. A good practice regimen is to take your bad shots to the driving range and overcome the faults that may creep into your game from time to time. Playing the game at any skill level requires the assumption that you have the capability to pull off the shot that you want in the circumstances. It requires that you take inventory of your skills and match those skills to the difficulty of the shot. You may have the skill to execute a particular shot, but if you believe you are incapable or you let negative thoughts creep into your psyche…invariably bad things will happen. In golf and in many sports, when bad things happen they seem to multiply, and therefore one bad shot will lead to another. You have to think that you have the skill, to pull yourself out of the spin. We've have seen these situations many times, particularly in competition and at the professional level. Under pressure, the game speeds up and disables the player's ability to draw upon the positive experiences of the past where focus on the fear of failure predominates the situation. This phenomenon occurs throughout the world of sport, but has a significant impact on the golfer, where individual performance under pressure is heightened.

Golf is a game where character is revealed. It's the only game where you compete against yourself in the company of others who are doing the same thing. It's amazing how people react in these circumstances. People with high handicaps often feel that they are not capable of playing with people with low handicaps. Handicapping is the great leveler of the golf game. Handicapping is another aspect of the ethics of the game of golf, as the individual is responsible for maintaining the golf handicap. There are rules that govern the maintenance of the golf handicap, but the basic premise is that the golf handicap enables players of all skill types to play together on a level playing field.

An example of this was a best ball match with my brother, who is a 15 handicap, against two other gentlemen in Connecticut. One player was an 8 handicap and the other was at least a 25. The 8 handicapper seemed to take the match very seriously and the 25 handicapper was a mess as his shots went all over the place and he lost a number of golf balls. We closed out the match on the 13th hole for 6 and 5 win, but there was little pleasure in it as the 25 handicapper shot over 110. The next day we were scheduled to play again, but the 8 handicapper had another venue and I invited the 25 handicapper to play with us again. He didn't want to play and he was clearly upset with his play. We told him to relax and join us and the next day we played a "skins" match with handicaps and he shot 97, winning most of the skins. A skins match is match where the best ball holed of the group wins a skin. If the hole is halved, meaning there was no best ball holed, then the "skin" is carried over until the hole is won.

The difference in these two days was on the second day. We thought it was important for the high handicapper to be comfortable and have fun than to press the game too seriously. We tried to play well and win but the 25 handicapper played better.

While the list may not be complete, the game of golf demonstrates traits of integrity, character, competiveness, and camaraderie unique in the world of sport.

Chapter 2
Getting Started

The motivation to write this book comes from a forty-year pursuit of the game of golf. As a child, boy, and young adult, golf was a television event for those afternoons when the Yankees were rained out. It was *Shell's Wonderful World of Golf* on the black and white screen from places unheard of, with rustic greens, polite crowds, and insipid commentary. People such as Bryon Nelson, Cary Middlecoff, Billy Casper were playing, and it was hard to understand the vagaries of the game watching it on television. Living in the inner city, there was no access to the game of golf. The New Haven Country Club was for very rich people and out of the economic potential of the middle class. In the inner city of New Haven, Connecticut there was no access to the game. I was raised in the Wooster Square section of the Italian part of town--a product of second-generation Italian immigrant parents with a father who somehow married into the clan. I was the only child in my grammar school of some 300 students whose name ended in a consonant. We spent our days playing football, baseball, and basketball on the church playgrounds and Wooster Square Park in New Haven, Connecticut which was all of 100 yards from our front door. We had eighteen boys in the neighborhood, so getting games pulled together was never a problem. However, getting picked to play was always a problem, so a competitive spirit was ignited very early in my life. Either perform well, or sit out, or don't play at all. Being the youngest of these eighteen boys made this a rather difficult task. The closest we ever came to the scent of green turf was attending Yale home football games at Yale Bowl where the local kids could get in for free as a "rope guard" that would prevent patrons from crossing into the reserved seats from general admission. Golf was Sam Snead, Byron Nelson, Gene Sarazin, and Arnold Palmer participating in *Shell's Wonderful World of Golf* television matches. The commentary of these matches seemed inane to me at the time and I had absolutely no feel for the skills required in the game.

All through grammar school and high school I pursued an athletic career in basketball and spent hours and hours at the game, hoping that one day my shot would be as good as Bill Bradley, my hero. No one in our family had ever gone to college and I was the first student to attend private Catholic high school in West Haven, Connecticut. Tuition was $250/yr. My family sacrificed so that I could attend the school, and I worked summers and during the school year while playing three sports in order to be able to buy books and have some spending money of my own. I was fortunate enough to move on to college and graduate with a degree in accounting, and after graduation I joined the public accounting firm of Peat, Marwick Mitchell & Co. (now called KPMG) and found myself in the business world.

The first golf experience was humbling and devastating. Having never picked up a golf club, I was at the Katonah Country Club in Westchester County, New York playing for the first time in the annual company golf tournament. I was twenty-four years old and attendance was required. I was paired in the last group with two women who also had never played the game before. It was a humbling experience and a calculator was required to compute the scores. I hit so many shots that I estimated my score:162. I was extremely frustrated with myself--no fundamentals—not even a basic grip. I can't even remember where the golf clubs came from. I was determined to improve and enjoy this game. The good shots I hit that day gave me the impression that it was possible and that I should continue to pursue this game. A set of of Jack Nicklaus McGregor clubs was immediately procured. Whacking thousands of golf balls would follow.

Initially success was rather limited, as I didn't take any lessons, but I was soon able to carve a swing that would enable me to get into the low 100s in a few months. I played public courses in Westchester County which were pretty nondescript and I can remember that most of these courses had no teeing ground and used the artificial turf found at most driving ranges. The golf bug bit me and we started planning our annual vacations around golf venues. In 1975 we started making annual treks to Hilton Head, South Carolina where I actually took my first lesson and started making some real progress. Progress was measured not in score, but the number of golf balls lost per round. In Hilton Head we stayed at the Palmetto Dunes resort which has 36 holes, consisting of one course designed by Robert Trent Jones and another designed by George Fazio. With all the water on these golf courses I went through a number of golf balls, but nevertheless came back encouraged.

The plight of taking up golf at age twenty-four is that you fall prey to all the traps of the beginning golfer at an age where all your memory is focused on negativity. Some of these traps are:

1. Poor fundamentals in the basic golf swing are accentuated by the memory that you have poor fundamentals and you're continuously talking yourself out of hitting the ball well.

2. A notion that everybody is watching you and is focused on your skill level and ability to hit the shot...as we all know now, nobody cares about your golf game and they just want you to hit the ball and get moving.
3. An inability to convert your shots on the driving range to the golf course, particularly in the area of putting and chipping.

Nevertheless, I persevered, playing bad golf on vacation and came home and joined Rye Golf Club in Rye, New York. The club was no more than ten minutes from our downtown Rye apartment.

We lived in Rye, New York and I set out to play public golf in Westchester County, New York. I was really horrible, spraying shots everywhere, and public golf in Westchester was a nauseating six- hour affair. I was getting nowhere, but I was persistent. Linda, as usual, was supportive, but I think she was worried I was going to kill somebody with my wayward shots or certainly do some serious damage. I was twenty-five years old and had spent most of my athletic life playing basketball and baseball, so I couldn't understand why I couldn't play this game. After all, it was just a game. We started to vacation every year at Hilton Head, South Carolina and it was there that I took my first golf lesson. I listened and practiced intently and I improved, but I was no match for the courses at Hilton Head. I hacked for a number of rounds, but good things were beginning to happen, at least from a ball-striking point of view. I had poor technique, such as a bounce and hitch to my swing with a bent left elbow...I would have to work on these things for many years afterward, but I was stuck with them at Hilton Head.

Nevertheless, I persevered and continued to play and practice at the Rye Golf Club. The club was five minutes from our apartment in Rye, which gave me the opportunity to place and practice at the semi-private facility. I didn't really keep a handicap, as I vacillated from the low 90s to the mid-100s. In 1978 we moved from Rye,

New York to our first home in Fairfield, Connecticut. I was working in New York City at the Singer Company at Rockefeller Center and commuting by train. We were focused on completing home improvements on our four-bedroom Colonial home, which was a real fixer-upper, so golf became a lower priority. The next eighteen months were wonderful as we spent many weekends with my in-laws at their home in Orange, Ct., which was a suburb of New Haven about 20 miles from Fairfield. My father-in-law, Dick, was a fairly good player—high 80s, low 90s--and we played together virtually every weekend during spring and summer at a public golf course not far from his home: Orange Hills Golf Club. Orange Hills is a basic public course with a pleasant layout and not very difficult, but well-kept and well-maintained. Most of the time we would just play nine holes on a late Sunday afternoon and enjoy each other's company. Dick Bowllan, my father-in-law, was a wonderful man and became a second father to me. He was left-handed and hit the ball pretty well, and for the next year was better than I was, at age fifty-eight. I didn't care, because I enjoyed his company so much. He loved the game of golf for what it was and he accepted the skills that he had at the game, without complaint. Of course he was always trying to improve, but those Sunday afternoons enabled us to develop a relationship that would stand the test of time until he died in 2001. We would play together when he later came to visit us in California as well as in England in 1991. He also played with his grandson, who would arrive on the scene in November, 1979.

Chapter 3
WEST COAST
MOVE--1979

In 1979 my career took me from New York City to the sunny confines of San Jose, California. It was a great move for us, but we were leaving our entire family behind in Connecticut, including our parents and all of our relatives.

We lived less than one mile from Almaden Country Club, a prestigious private club in San Jose where the initiation membership was $30,000. It could have been a million as far as I was concerned, since we could barely afford our house payment. As a result, it was a life of public golf, only this time there were few places to play and the courses were pretty sad. I played and practiced at public facilities where rounds lasted from six to six and a half hours. In 1979, San Jose was booming in real estate due to the significant success of the technology markets in semiconductors, computers, and software. There were few golf courses and this was true not only for San Jose, but for the entire Bay Area. One very nice course was Santa Teresa Golf Club in south San Jose which I played often, but it was an all-day affair, which was very difficult with a young son.

Ian was barely three years old at the time. My game was not improving under these conditions and I was playing in the high nineties and low 100s. For me the years 1979-1985 were dark golf years as I plodded along in frustration through the morass of public golf in the Bay Area. I know these words are "snooty" and "arrogant," but I've never understood why Americans play the game so slowly on public golf courses. Part of the problem is the manner in which the courses are managed, sending foursomes off every six minutes, which ends up creating a natural traffic jam just like any freeway. For the public course operation, it's a matter of dollars and cents and who cares if the customer enjoys it or not. This is not just a Bay Area phenomenon but a truly global one as I had similar experiences in France, England, Portugal, China, and Hawaii.

In 1981 I introduced the game of golf to my son, Ian, who was six. This was the best things I have ever done and my relationship with my son has been nurtured and fostered throughout the last thirty-four years together on the golf course. We have covered the facts of life-- teachers, girlfriends, cars, job, fiancées--on the course together in ways we couldn't have otherwise accomplished. On a Saturday he would learn the golf swing properly (not from me) from the resident professional. He gave Ian and the rest of the kids lessons not only in the golf swing, but how to enjoy and respect the game. These are lessons that have stuck with us over these past thirty-four years. He spent one hour per week on the range at age six, repeating and practicing. At the age of eight, Ian had his introduction to the Oakridge Golf Course (now part of California Highway 85) playing from the ladies' tees with his peers on a Sunday afternoon. He enjoyed himself and today still has a great swing and technique.

From 1979 to 1981, I continued to focus mostly on practicing and playing a little and taking Ian out with me. I really didn't have any goals for myself or my game. In 1982, my daughter Meredith was born and we were transferred to San Rafael, California. We bought a home on the Marin Country Club grounds just off the 6th tee. The closest I ever got to playing Marin Country Club was hitting wedges from my back yard onto the 6th fairway. My golfing days were limited to playing Indian Valley Golf Club in Novato. The winter of 1982 was one of the wettest winters on record, so we sloshed around in the mud most weekends there.

Chapter 4
LESSONS--DEBACLE

In 1984 and I wasn't getting any better. I was still playing public golf as a member of the Men's Club at Riverside Golf Club in South San Jose. We played in a group every weekend and it was getting tiresome. I decided that I would take lessons from the Riverside resident professional. This turned out to be a very bad decision. The pro asked me what my goals were and I said I wanted to get to a single-digit handicap and get rid of all of the accumulated faults that my golf swing had developed in the past twelve years. He decided that everything in my golf swing and approach would have to change—the hitch, the bent elbow, and a bunch of other things. My game went completely to pieces to the point that I could not hit a golf ball 10 yards. Whatever the pro was telling me, I wasn't executing it and the bad shots multiplied in a geometric progression. Negative thoughts prevailed in everything that I tried to do, and I couldn't gain any confidence with any of the changes. There were so many things to change that I couldn't execute any of them. I couldn't play with my friends anymore because it was too embarrassing. I decided two things:

1. I had to stop the lessons--they were killing me.
2. I had to stop playing completely --it was killing me

So in the summer of 1984, I stopped playing completely—no driving range, no golf course, nothing. I was disappointed, but I had two wonderful young children to be with and I decided to spend the summer with them. I started watching a lot of golf on television, trying to pick up some things that I could try. The tempo that the professional has is truly remarkable, and I saw a number of swings that I decided to try to emulate. I picked up a drill watching Fred Couples swing effortlessly with his left hand only before he hit a shot. I have maintained that drill in my game since 1985. The left side is very important to the golf swing, as most amateur players can't get the concept of weight shifting to finish high and maximize their power. I took the entire summer off and that particular summer, my close friend and golf partner had the summer of his life in golf. He was a 15 handicap and we played together at Riverside every Saturday in the same foursome. As I had to give up since I couldn't keep up with the group, he started playing in the low 80s and high 70s and won virtually every competition he entered that summer. My loss was his gain. As the summer ended and the crisp fall air began to descend on northern California, I decided to give it a try and head for the driving range. I didn't know what to expect. I had a feeling that the demons had left me. The negative thoughts from the lessons and memories of the Riverside professional had faded. I had confidence and was really focused on tempo. I started hitting balls and all of sudden, it was all there, iron shots were going straight and true with a slight fade from pitching wedge to 3 iron. The woods were decent. I had developed a fade, striking the ball from out to in--which is not ideal, but not horrible. I wasn't slicing the ball and contact was terrific. I decided to start playing again in the late- November timeframe and made the progress I was hoping to make when I had decided to take lessons at Riverside. Almost immediately my scores were reduced to the mid to high 80s and my handicap started to plummet. Before the summer swoon of 1984, my handicap was 18 and by summer of 1985, it was down to a consistent 12. I guess there may be something to watching golf on television. I always marvel at the plethora of golf instruction on TV and in the golf magazines, as if somehow you are going to learn something from one of these publications and take it to the golf course. I think most of it is rubbish, but it is entertaining. Golfers are always looking for the tip and the shortcut that is going to accelerate their improvement. The problem with golf is that once you think you have something fixed with your swing, something else--such as putting and chipping--deteriorates and your attention is diverted to those areas. I believe that the following ideas helped me get through the swoon and come out the other side without lessons.

1. Focus...for me, focus is trying to develop the muscle memory required to hit good shots time after time.
2. Forget the bad shots and remember the good ones and always try to repeat them by remembering how they happened. I believe if you focus on bad shots and get angry and upset, the bad shots will keep coming and you'll never achieve the opportunity to improve.
3. Practice, practice, practice...all aspects of the game, but spend a lot of time on the short game. 40% of the game is in this category. Count putts, greens in regulation, and sand saves, and set goals for performance. Focus on the short game and try to achieve fewer than thirty putts per round and have a bunker/save percentage of 50%.

The summer of 1984 was the nadir of my golf game and the spring of 1985 was the beginning of a renaissance where I could continue to build a foundation for my golf game. In 1985, I had marked a little over ten years with golf, and I was determined to get better.

Chapter 5
AMATEURS AND PROFESSIONALS

It's important to understand that professionals possess all the skills necessary in their golf swing, or they could never achieve that status. The professional's golf swing is created by club head speed at impact which determines length and accuracy. There is a lot of discussion today about equipment and the golf ball. Amateurs often don't see the benefits of the equipment and golf ball because their club head speed cannot approach that of the professional player. Professionals certainly have various techniques and differences in their swings, takeaways, turns, etc. but they strike the ball at impact and at a club head speed with consistency that cannot be duplicated by the amateur. It doesn't matter how tall, how muscular, or how heavy the player is; club head speed through the ball is what matters. Tom Watson still drives the ball today 280 yards at the age of sixty-two today because he can still generate significant club head speed and take advantage of the ball and the equipment. He also has one of the purest golf swings of all time.

Chapter 6
EXPERIENCES

AUGUSTA NATIONAL GOLF CLUB

It was April of 2003 and I was pretty excited. I had been invited to come to Augusta National Golf Club for a three-day weekend. The timing was the end of May, 2003 and the Masters had just been played there some weeks earlier. There were forces, however, working against me getting there. In addition to issues at work I had received a notice in the mail summoning me for jury duty. There was no way that jury duty was going to prevent me from going to Augusta. I conjured up a written note from my boss, the CEO, and off I went to the San Jose courthouse to plead my case. I had a business meeting in Atlanta, Georgia that had been scheduled for at least a month predating this jury duty notice. The court clerk looked up at me with disdain as if she had heard it all before as I pleaded my case for exclusion. She told me I would have to talk the judge with the rest of the draftees. I was prepared for anything as I approached the bench. I showed her the letter, the airline tickets (I was leaving the next day) and stated how important this meeting was to the company. The judge looked at me with utter disgust and lit into me as if I were about to stand trial myself. The judge went into a mini tirade about what a miserable human being I was for not supporting the system. "Get out of here, you miserable excuse for a human being," she exclaimed. I simply put my head down and enjoyed the beating. Thank you, God, I'm outta here and off to Augusta.

It was an early Thursday morning and the first stop was Los Angeles for the Jacobs Engineering board meeting. By 4:00 p.m. I would be flying out of Los Angeles direct to Atlanta and on to Augusta for a mid-morning tee time. Of course I entered the board room at Jacobs bragging about my good fortune as to where my next stop was. Many of the directors were avid golfers and I was the envy of that day. I was off to the airport at 1:30 p.m. with my clubs in tow. I never bring golf clubs with me when I travel to play in other parts of the US, but this was too special. I had to have my own sticks. I tipped the skycap a clean crisp $20 when he checked my golf bag to ensure that it would meet its intended destination in Augusta and off I went. After a smooth five- hour Delta flight to Atlanta, I was getting excited. My excitement would be short-lived as my clubs were nowhere to be found as I went to retrieve them at baggage claim. How could this be? A direct flight, no issues, no diversions, a $20 tip!—how could the clubs be lost?? They were indeed "lost" and "expletives deleted," I boarded the connecting flight to Augusta without clubs, but with my spirits deflated. Delta dutifully started the search for the clubs and promised to get them to me on the first available flight. Later I would find out that my clubs went to Hawaii instead of Atlanta—so much for the $20 tip. In any event I showed up and went rolling down Magnolia Lane. I was psyched, clubs or no clubs. Staying at the club is a treat in itself. It is not ostentatious, but very cozy and comfortable. We had a mid- morning tee time, and I was going to have play with whatever golf clubs Augusta National had available for me. My ticket to this wonderful invitation was the former chairman of Ford Motor Company, who had invested in a venture fund with me. We were joined by his friend, a self-made millionaire, from Palm Beach and a member of Palm Beach Country Club (a Bernie Madoff hunting ground) and young banker from Texas. I had the best game of the group, but the young banker was a terrific long hitter who could play quite well.

Being on the driving range that first day was very special when I thought of the players that preceded me. I was given a set of clubs by the pro shop and off we went. The fabulous thing was the caddies. We would have four caddies for all three days, and they would be the same caddy for all three days. Believe me, without the caddies, putting would have been impossible since it is not possible to read the Augusta greens. The greens were like glass, fresh from the Masters, and we were playing the same pin positions as the professionals. We were not playing the professional yardages. New tees had been installed to push the course to over 7,200 yards. We played the course at about 6,500 yards. Augusta National is spectacular and television is no substitute for the beauty of the course. I simply enjoyed the walk and did the best I could that first day with the borrowed clubs. I shot 85, which was respectable, but the score was way off my handicap. I couldn't adjust to the wedges and putter that were provided, and threw some shots away. No excuses! I struck the ball reasonably well and got a feel for the course, and improvement would come in the ensuing two days, particularly on Sunday (our last round). Of course we went to the pro shop after the round to stock up on Augusta and Masters merchandise and memorabilia. I had attended the Masters event a number of times and had a good deal of the stuff. While I would spend some money, I wasn't going to max out my credit card there. Our man from Palm

Beach went on a tear…he bought everything in sight from cocktail glasses to placemats and everything that had a "Masters" logo on it. The professional would have to restock the shop after he left I estimate that over $5,000 or more was spent in that afternoon. We had a wonderful dinner that Friday night and got to visit the Perch (where the juniors sleep) and other places around the club. It was magical for a golfer and the service was impeccable. It was a memorable evening of Georgian hospitality.

My thoughts turned to Delta Airlines and the status of my clubs. I got good news: the clubs had been located in Hawaii and they would arrive in Augusta by 9:00 Saturday morning-- and they did. I was really hyped up to play that Saturday on a sunny hot humid day with a gentle Georgian breeze. Off we went and I parred the difficult first hole and started to strike it pretty well. Thanks to the caddies, I made some great putts and got round in 79. I never did conquer the 18th hole, as I had a double bogey there every day. I just kept driving it into the pine straw to the right of the fairway and could never get close enough to do any better. I had birdies on the 8th and the 15th and had a generally satisfying round. We spent another pleasurable evening, and yes, our man from Palm Beach did go back and buy even more stuff from the freshly stocked pro shop. It was amazing to watch.

Sunday turned out to be very special. After playing two consecutive days in sunny, hot, humid weather, you are definitely warmed up and without excuses. I was on fire and completed the front nine in 37 with nothing very spectacular. The fun would start on the infamous 12th hole over Rae's Creek. My tee shot crossed the creek and landed in the back of the green some 35 feet from the hole. I was elated to be on the green and the pin was in the normal Sunday position which is just a few paces from the down slope that heads into the creek. I had an interesting 35-foot putt downhill and lightning fast. The caddie showed me a line and I carefully pulled back on the Odyssey straight and true and it trickled and trickled and boom...found the bottom of the hole for a 2. I was jumping for joy, having accomplished something I never dreamed of and the caddy recorded the event with my digital camera. The photograph is framed and is displayed in my home today. Off to the par 5 13th hole with Rae's Creek guarding the green...it is the Hades of the golfing gods and has consumed the likes of Curtis Strange, Phil Mickelson, Fred Couples, and countless others trying to cross it in 2 and make an eagle. My drive was straight and true down the middle about 225 yards where the luxury of being a short driver makes you aware that you could never reach the green in 2. I proceeded to take a 5 iron and hit it straight down the middle 175 yards for my second shot. I would have a 90-yard approach shot to the green over the creek. Nerves were rattling. I struggled with removing the negative thoughts from my brain that I would somehow dump this shot into the creek. I managed to overcome these thoughts, but I hit it a little too long and found myself some 50 feet from the Sunday pin position, which is placed about 3 yards from the creek. More negative thoughts--conceivably a poor effort that was too hard could result in a putt that could end up in the creek. Once again the caddie gave me the line and once again the Odyssey went straight back and boom--it's in Hole-Birdie 4. It was my fourth birdie of the day and I couldn't believe it--and neither could anyone else. On to 14!

Now I was thoroughly pumped up and we were playing the 14th from about 360 yards—the professionals play the hole from 440 yards now. The 14th is an absolutely beautiful hole, shaped by magnolia trees, with a reasonably generous fairway. The issue on 14 is the treacherous green with all of its undulations, which no one can appreciate from watching on television. I had my tee shot right down the middle again about 200 yards—not very long...

it felt good, but it went nowhere. But I was in the middle of the fairway. I chose another 5 iron as there was a bit of wind and I wanted to carry the shot all the way to the hole. I flushed it and looked great in the air and it almost went in and stopped about a foot away from the hole. Another birdie…this time a NPR or (no putter required). I tapped it in with the 5 iron for yet another birdie. What's all this stuff about AMEN Corner? We conquered it on that Sunday. Of course I made 6 again on the 18th for a 1 over 73 with five birdies, six bogeys and seven pars. I made sure that the score card was signed and it sits framed today in my den in San Jose…dubbed the "golf man cave" by my close friends.

After the round we had a short libation and then it was off to the Par 3 course, caddies in tow. I don't remember much about the Par 3 course. It's like playing the 12th hole nine times. The course is carved around a pond so water is in play on virtually every hole. We decided to play a skins game and I won eight skins in the competition, mostly on carryovers. Of course nobody cares or remembers about that bet but the company and the ambience of the layout was great fun. What a finish to a glorious golfing weekend, never to be forgotten, and shared here.

What I took away from Augusta National was the simplicity and unpretentious nature of the club. It simply reeks of class and love for the game, where everyone is there for a good time. It's the closest thing to heaven on earth for the pure pleasure of the game.

THE MASTERS MYSTIQUE

I've attended the Masters as a spectator many times and it is a wonderful experience. The event is highly differentiated from all others on the PGA Tour. The event is carefully staged and I call it an "egalitarian affair" since there are no corporate hospitality tents, logos, or preferred seating. You get to the course and you partake in a great event. There is no yelling "You the Man" or "John 3:16" signs over the course. There is no advertising. You don't have to spend $100 feeding yourself at this event, as you are efficiently served with a ham and cheese sandwich, or a cheese and pickle sandwich which sell for $1.50. You can feed twenty people here for the price of what you'll pay at any other PGA event. If you are caught with a cell phone, you will be escorted out of the gates without exception. One of the really unique things here is that you can purchase you own folding chair. You can place this chair anywhere outside the ropes on the course and it will never be touched or moved by another spectator. You leave the chair at your strategic spot and then you can walk the entire course at your pace and leisure and when you want to sit in that chair, you will always find it unoccupied and unmoved. Any other event would have this chair stolen for sure.

The merchandise kiosk is very special and their system is easy to maneuver. Masters golf gear is special and cannot be purchased outside the grounds or online. You buy it because it tells people that you've been there, because that's the only way you can get it. The merchandise tent is crowded but efficient, as only a fixed number of people are allowed in at any one time, but the tent is well-staffed with courteous people and the lines move smoothly. Once you've completed your conspicuous consumption, you don't have to tote it around…which of course means you can buy as much as you want. Once you leave the tent, Fed Ex is right around the corner to ship your merchandise home without a care in the world. The place simply exudes class in everything that it does for this prestigious event.

The tournament is the most pleasurable experience that a spectator can have at a golf event. I always placed my chair in the front row on the 16th hole Par 3, provided I arrived soon enough to gain that position. After walking the golf course for most of the day I came back to the 16th hole and found my chair untouched and unoccupied. An improbable happening--can you imagine doing something like that at the Phoenix Open?

RYDER CUP

The Ryder Cup matches are golf at its purest state: match play, which is the ultimate in competition, especially amongst the world's best players. The matches pit the best players in the United States against the best players from Europe. The players qualify for the event through their standing on the respective professional tour. The captain of the team is selected by the respective PGA organization and the captain is given one discretionary selection for a team member. The best part about the current state of the competition is the strength of the US and European teams is pretty close, which makes for fabulous golf and excitement. I've always been interested in the quality of the matches rather than who actually wins. The original intent of Samuel Ryder was to promote a "friendly" competition of the best players from the United States, and Great Britain and Ireland. The competition was one sided for many years due to the depth of the US team with only so many world-class players available. When the Europeans were added to the squad in 1976, the situation turned significantly as the European side dominated the matches for a number of events led by swashbuckler Seve Ballesteros. The Europeans were no longer cannon fodder for the US PGA stars, and interest in the event became rather hysterical. The event turned into a jingoistic affair with fans on both sides displaying significant bad behavior. After a series of stunning US defeats, the venue became the "war by the shore" at Kiawah Island, South Carolina in 1996 with the US team captained by Dave Stockton. This was a "must" win for the beleaguered US side and after three fabulous days of puts and takes, it all came down to the 18th hole in the match between Bernard Langer and Hale Irwin. The pressure on both men was incredible as they proceeded to the tough 18th hole. Irwin's drive went way left into the crowd, and I am convinced to this day that this ball was given a fairly healthy kick back into the light rough when it was probably "almost dead." We all know the result, with Langer missing a six- foot putt to halve the matches, but it was not an easy putt. The display that followed the US victory became a symbol and rallying cry for future games, and you would think that this was the biggest victory since the signing of the Declaration of Independence in 1776. The matches have now taken a nationalistic tone and hype following this victory. Crowds now tend to be partisan and sometimes rude to the participants. The behavior of the US team following Justin Leonard's winning putt in the 2002 event at the Country Club in Massachusetts was appalling as his opponent, Jose Maria Olazabal, still had a putt to halve the hole (difficult as it was). The emotional part of the event seems to have ebbed a bit, but not enough to resume the original spirit of the event that Samuel Ryder intended.

There is a lot of pressure on the team captains. The captains are essentially filling out lineup cards for the best golfers in the world. It's not like baseball where managers have to strategize their position players. The skill of the captain is his intuition about how to assess the physical and mental condition of the player and to place him in the lineup where he can be the most effective. The captain also has to deal with ensuring that the players come together as a team and collaborate and encourage their peers. It's also important to ensure that the operational side of the event is well managed from a logistical standpoint so that the players can stay focused on the competition.

In recent years, the European team has done the better job of presenting itself as a team. The Europeans tend to play together and play superior golf in team formats such as foursomes and alternative match play. The US tends to dominate in the singles matches, which account for half the point potential in the matches and are always played on the final day of the matches.

Fast forward to 2010 and the Cup was played at Celtic Manor in Wales captained by Colin Montgomerie (Europe) and Corey Pavin (US). The squads seemed to be pretty evenly matched, with a mixture of first-timers who earned their way in, and grizzled professionals. Tiger Woods limped into this event with his game in tatters as a Captain's Pick. His No. 1 in the world ranking and his impressive list of accomplishments required that he be on the team. Phil Mickelson came into this event playing poorly, unable to overtake Tiger with shoddy play in the Fed Ex Cup competition. A great Captain's Pick was swashbuckling Rickie Fowler who hadn't yet won on the PGA Tour but has a no-fear approach to the game. The Europeans would also be without some familiar faces. Sergio Garcia failed to qualify and was not selected as a Captain's Pick despite his terrific Ryder Cup record and leadership. He joined Monty's staff as a Vice Captain (professional helper). A more controversial slight was Paul Casey, ranked No. 7 in the world, and also left off the team. The stage was set for an interesting event and both captains handled their squads differently but I felt this cup was played under the guidance of Samuel Ryder himself. Despite the natural jingoist tendencies of the home crowd, there seemed to be a terrific amount of mutual respect for the capabilities of each squad. The result was close all the way with the Europeans bringing back the cup to Europe with a one-point victory, which wasn't settled until the last match on the 16th hole as the reigning US Open champion, Grahame McDowell completed a 3-1 victory over Hunter Mahan. The US had been down 9 ½ to 6 ½ going into the singles competition and it seemed a long uphill climb for the Americans, but they made a real run at it. Rickie Fowler earned a halved match with stellar play down the stretch after being way down in the match. Steve Stricker dispatched Europe's best player Lee Westwood and Tiger won easily over rookie Francisco Molinari. The matches were well played all week as the players endured difficult rainy conditions, play stoppages, and scheduling havoc. The US team's raingear and golf bags leaked, leading to some embarrassment and harried trips to the pro shop. To his credit, Pavin did not whine or complain about the conditions, as he stated correctly that the conditions were the same for everybody and you just had to go out and play and win your matches. If Pavin was analytical or intense, he didn't let it get across to the media. Asked how the US could recover on the final day, he stated in Yogi Berra-like parlance that his players would have to play better. I found his attitude very refreshing from the normal hype. I was genuinely pleased with the sportsmanship offered by this event after all the years preceding it of partisanship. Bottom line…these players on both sides are very good and basically dead even, capable of beating anyone on a given day. It seems that while the players really feel the pressure…they seem to know how to handle it. McDowell stated that the pressure was so bad coming down the 16th hole that he compared his walk down the 18th hole at the US Open at Pebble Beach as playing with his father on a Sunday afternoon. I was struck by how both sides handled the pressure with recoveries after missed putts and some truly imaginative shots. They were also human and hit a bunch of bad shots and missed putts as well—the Americans just a few more than the Europeans.

I had the opportunity to play Celtic Manor in April 2010 and wasn't terribly impressed with the venue. The course is a parkland venue and was set up to be very long--over 7,400 yards. I still believed that these players would put up a lot of birdies, and they did, but the wet conditions prevented the greens from being very fast, which enabled the players to go flag hunting. We played the course from about 7,000 yards, which was far shorter and particularly the par 3s were a lot easier for us with all the water in play, but these holes were over 200 yards for the event. We used a driver and two three woods to reach the 615 yard 9th hole. I didn't like the 15th hole, but I knew it was going to be a great hole for the professionals. The 15th is a drivable par 4 of 350 yards with a green surrounded by heavy spinachy rough, and bunkers guarded by a stream. The drive had to be hit precisely to navigate the tree line, which was the angle to the hole. The players made many birdies on this hole, but it was very competitive, particularly in the four-ball matches, since if both players on a team missed the green, it was almost certainly a lost hole. The real fun was the 575 yard 18th hole with a slightly elevated green. The green was guarded by a pond and the rough was shaved bald so that any shot short of the pin with any spin at all would end up in the water. The hole was a perfect climax if the matches were close, as the excitement of the approach shot was tantalizing. Stewart Cink and Rory McElroy hit terrific drives and decided to go for the green in two and both hit terrific shots that landed on the green, but alas, spun back into the pond. Brian and I hit terrific drives (for us) and laid up to 100 yards. I hit a pitching wedge past the flag-50 feet-two putted and enjoyed the par and the round.

The Celtic Manor was a typical British golf resort and built for this event. The hotel and restaurant were quite good and there are other courses there that reminded me of the typical British parkland course.

GOLF RULES HORROR-PGA CHAMPIONSHIP, AUGUST 15, 2010

An exciting tournament comes down to the last hole with the leader, Dustin Johnson, ahead by one shot teeing off on the treacherous 18th hole at Whistling Straits. Johnson is pumped and knows how to play it only one way, and that it is to rip it and take advantage of his length on this 514-yard par 4. Well--he rips, all right, but the club face is slightly open at impact and off to the right it heads right into the crowd. He's crushed it over 280 yards, but as the crowd separates and probably places the ball, he is left in a pile of sand some 231 yards from the hole. Here is where things get foggy and where tournament management failed. Johnson had to deal with getting the crowd out of the way so that he could even address the ball as he was surrounded by the screaming gallery. Galleries today are not what they used to be, as they will distract the player rather than get out of his way. Each pairing in a tournament is supposed to be accompanied by rules officials, but there was no official to be seen. It wasn't obvious that this pile of sand outside the ropes was a fairway bunker. No one saw any rules official telling Dustin that this was a bunker, and it seemed that his caddy was confused as well. The "bunker" had been trampled down by the crowd; it simply looked like a pile of plain sand. The lip of the bunker had also been trampled down as well. When you play major championships, you would think that bunker identification is one of the easiest things to figure out. Well either Dustin didn't realize it or he just made an error, but he did ground his club as he connected with the ball and sent it some 230 yards left of the green in another sea of grass and trouble. He wasn't able to get up and down from there and recorded a bogey, or so he thought.

As he left the green getting mentally ready for a three-hole playoff with Martin Kaymer and Bubba Watson, a rules official came up to him and told him he had a problem. Thanks for nothing. *Where were you when I needed you before I hit the shot?* is the thought that must have gone through Dustin's mind. The rules official told him that he had grounded the club in what was indeed a fairway bunker and therefore he incurred a two-shot penalty. After a fifteen-minute harangue, Dustin gave up in frustration and signed his card with the penalty, disqualifying him from the playoff and ending up with a triple bogey 7 instead of a bogey 5, dropping him nearly out of the top ten finishers at -9 for the tournament. When questioned by TV commentators, the rules official helpfully noted that the players were warned with written notices before tournament play that there were all sorts of bunkers out of play on the Whistling Straits layout. Of course Dustin should have remembered this written notice, probably posted in the men's dressing room latrine on Wednesday, as he contemplated hitting a 231-yard shot to win the PGA Championship. There should have been a rules official present and he should have informed Dustin and his caddy that this pile of trodden soil was indeed a bunker and to be careful when addressing the ball. His caddie should also have known what was going on, but he too was caught in the moment of trying to help his man with a very difficult shot. It was strange ending to a terrific golf course whose reputation in my mind will be stained by this silly situation, which may have cost Dustin Johnson the PGA Championship. The opportunity to win a major championship doesn't happen often...just ask Scott Hoch about Augusta National. Hoch missed a two-foot putt on the 18th hole at Augusta and eventually lost the tournament to Nick Faldo.

GOLF TALES

It was one of those days when you play golf for business purposes and on this particular Sunday, the venue was Blackhawk Country Club in Danville, California. The participants included me, our

Japanese business manager, our head of operations, and the general manager of the business unit. Blackhawk was the general manager's home course and he also resided there. He is an avid golfer and has played everywhere—a real gentleman and a fine businessman. The Japanese executive had just arrived from Japan and our Japanese executives were also keen players who always played on weekends when they were in the US.

Blackhawk is rather nondescript and I really can't remember much about the course now since I haven't played it since, but this day would produce one of the most embarrassing moments in golf that I have ever experienced. The only thing that I recollect about the course is that it is a typical US golf course development community, but the homes hug many of the fairways on either side. This was a fairly competent foursome, so we should have gotten through the day routinely.

Our trouble started early in the round. We reached the third hole which was a straightaway par 4 of 380 yards or so. The right side of the fairway about 80 yards stood a series of homes. Two of us hit tee shots into the middle of the fairway and the general manager sliced one to the right about 15 yards to the right but in playable condition. The Japanese executive got up and sliced a drive way right and high and then we heard a horrific crash and the horrible sound of breaking glass. One of the homes had been hit, and the occupants were home and scurrying for cover as screams emanated from the abode. The Japanese executive looked up in disbelief and was totally crushed as to what he has just accomplished—he had broken a window.

The general manager turned to us calmly and said, "Don't worry, I have homeowner's insurance and I will take care of this."

He dutifully marched to the home that had just been violated and the owner was standing there waiting and we didn't know what to expect. The general manager disarmed the situation with his patience and class and apologized to the homeowner and told him that he would pay for the damage, and proceeded to give the homeowner the details of how he could be reached. It almost reminded me of the scene of a traffic accident.

In any event, all was well and we were ready to play on after twenty minutes or so--fortunately Blackhawk is a private club and there were no groups following us that day. Okay, a broken window—it's happened thousands of times to golfers and homeowners, so what's the big deal? What happened next was the big deal…the general manager went up to his ball and hit something like a five-iron and sliced it way right. High in the air. I grimaced, "NOOOOOOO!"

But yes!!!

Another home 50 yards up the fairway—crash!!!……another broken window. What are the odds for two different players to hit consecutive golf shots that will result in a broken window? The chances are pretty low…first of all you have houses close to the fairways; second, you have to have very poor golf shots and third, they have to be consecutive golf shots by different players. The two of us in the fairway looked at each other and said absolutely nothing. This shot had a devastating impact on the Japanese executive, and it just brought back the horrible nightmare to his immediate attention. The general manager, however, was nonplussed. He simply began his lumbering march to the impacted home where the owner was waiting. Again he apologized profusely to the owner and stated that he was a club member and homeowner at Blackhawk and he would dutifully pay for the damages of his strike. The two of us who had managed not to break any windows remained in the fairway and had not hit our second shots.

Almost forty minutes had passed and two consecutive shots had resulted in property damage to homes on the golf courses. I turned to the group and stated, "I don't know about you guys, but I'm using my putter from here."

THE FIRST EXPERIENCE AT THE OLD COURSE AT ST. ANDREWS

This story could be labeled as a fable out of *Ripley's "Believe It or Not"* as it relates to my first playing experience at the Old Course at St. Andrews. The year was 1985 and I was alone on a business trip that would start in Amsterdam, Holland where the company had its European headquarters. The visit would start at mid-week and then continue at the company's semiconductor equipment division in Horsham, England about sixty miles north of London in the county of West Sussex. The question was, what was I going to do for the weekend. I was relatively new to the company, so I had no friends in Amsterdam or England at the time. It just jumped into my head—*Why not fly from Amsterdam to Edinburgh and see whether I can see St. Andrews?* I had no idea regarding the geography of Scotland and I had never been there before. There was good flight service out of Amsterdam to Edinburgh and I made a reservation at the Caledonian Hotel right across the street from Edinburgh Castle in downtown Edinburgh. I flew out on a Friday night flight on something called Air UK--called YUK by the locals--but it was fine and I landed at the airport and proceeded by taxi to the hotel. I got up early the next morning and proceeded to the front desk and asked the concierge how to get to St. Andrews. Could I take a cab? I thought it was close by. The concierge asked me if I drove a car and I said that I was an American and had no idea as to how to drive on the right-hand side of the road, and furthermore had no idea of where I was going, so driving was out of the question. He proceeded to direct me to Scottish Rail and told me that the train did not go all the way to St. Andrews and that I needed to get off at a certain town whose name escapes me. He then told me I could then take a cab the rest of the way to the Old Course at St. Andrews, which is right in the middle of the town.

I followed his directions and took a cab to the Old Course. Along the way I decided that I was going to do anything to try and actually play the Old Course. I didn't quite understand how I was going to do this, since I had no golf clubs, no golf shoes, and no golf attire. Nevertheless, I decided that I would figure it all out when I got there. It was a cold, damp and gray typical Scottish day in the second week of November. There is a street that you turn on to and pass the 18th hole with the Royal and Ancient Club building on the right as you turn in. The pro shop and starter's shed and first tee are on the left side of the street, and the street ends at the beach at the Firth of Forth. It was about 10 a.m. when we turned onto that street, and I asked the cab driver if he would return at 5 p.m. to pick me up and take me back to the rail station for the return trip to Edinburgh. He dropped me off at the telephone booth right outside the 18th. Of course it was a traditional old fire-engine red British Telecom booth (rotary dial, of course). I didn't know how to use a phone and I didn't even leave the cabbie any details. He told me that he would pick me up and I just trusted him to do so at 5 p.m. It would be dark by then for sure as dusk arrived in Scotland at 4 p.m. in the November time frame.

I then proceeded with my plan into the pro shop, where there were no customers and only a gentle, engaging man who asked me if he could help me. I told him I wanted to play the course and that I was a crazy American who had come all the way from California through Amsterdam, Holland, to Scotland to realize a lifelong dream to play the Old Course. He looked at me and said pretty nonchalantly that there was a group going off in about twenty minutes and I could join them if I wished. I got very excited and told him I had no golf clubs, no golf shoes or any golfing attire.

He told me, "No problem--we have clubs for you, and as for the rest, the golf shop is just across the way and you can get whatever you need there."

I got really excited now and went into the Old Tom Morris Golf Shop and proceeded to buy golf shoes (yes, with spikes), shirt, sweater, rain jacket and hat, golf gloves, etc. and went charging back into the pro shop. The greens fee was 15 pound sterling and off I went and joined the threesome and had the time of my life out there. I rented a set of clubs and without any warmup proceeded to tee it up on the first hole, which may be the widest fairway of any golf course I had ever played or would play. I was so excited I had a hard time remembering what I had done…all I remember about the round was the friendliness and camaraderie of my fellow players. They were three local Scotsmen who simply welcomed me into their afternoon at St. Andrews. They were amazed that I had come this far to play the course. It was a cold gray day in 1985 and the wind was howling, but we somehow kept warm and the group proceeded to walk me through the paces of the course.

These were the days when St. Andrews could be played anytime-- before the lottery and the New Hotel. The 17th (the Road Hole), the most difficult par 4 perhaps in all of golf, was flanked by the railway not the New Hotel. I had a glorious day on the course and felt as if I had accomplished something very special and rather crazy given the circumstances. We were finished by 3:30 p.m. and retreated to the bar at the Rasher's Hotel, which adjoins the 18th hole. One of the interesting parts about playing St. Andrew's is that it is actually in the middle of the town, so you start to acquire a "gallery" of onlookers as you head for home from the 15th hole on in. People strolling about with their children some of them engaged in kite-flying on that gray day in November. Amazingly, the same taxi driver who brought me to the course from the train station dutifully picked me up at 5 p.m. at the big red British Telecom phone booth and took me back to the train station.

I would come back to play St. Andrews another dozen times or so, but nothing was as special as the first time. It was an improbable happening and something that could never be done today. Today, the Old Course is as busy as Pebble Beach, with groups from around the world teeing off every ten minutes from the crack of dawn to dusk.

IAN AND I PLAY THE OLD COURSE AT ST. ANDREWS FOR THE FIRST TIME

When we lived in England, we had the good fortune of being able to take holiday breaks, as the Brits called them, which usually meant Thursday through Sunday or Friday through Sunday (a long weekend in the United States). One such break was taken with the family in Edinburgh and we stayed at the Caledonian Hotel, which is just across the street from Edinburgh Castle. Ian was eleven years old. He had been taking golf lessons since he was six years old at a driving range in San Jose. At age nine, he was playing the golf course and making great progress. We were playing with one of our Scottish salesmen who lived outside of Edinburgh. He was a good player and the three of us set out for the pro shop to register for the round. It was a glorious sunny day for Scotland—crisp, with the usual wind. As we walked into the starter's office the starter cast a menacing look at Ian and asked him for his handicap certificate. We had been warned about the potential of this occurring at the Old Course, so I immediately whisked out a piece of paper signed by the club professional at Almaden Country Club that Ian's handicap was nine. The starter had to accept this certification and off we went to the first tee where Ian blasted a picture- perfect drive down the first fairway just short of the Swilcan Burn, where most professionals hit it. Ian went round the course that day with a round of 81 and at 4'11" disappeared from sight on a few occasions in the Hell

Bunker on number 14 and a few of the pot bunkers on the front nine. It was an exciting experience for both of us playing together at the Old Course.

THE OLD COURSE AS A BRITISH OPEN VENUE

The British Open returned to the Old Course at St. Andrews in 2010, and it is a very special venue. Unfortunately the course has passed its prime for being a difficult test for the modern game. Tom Watson said it best, "Stay out of the bunkers," and putting will determine the winner. The course is utterly defenseless against the modern professional who can strike the golf ball 300 yards plus. The course was lengthened to slightly over 7,300 yards, but its fast fairways and lack of rough posed no difficulty to the field as the cut line was only 3 over par. This is a course with absolutely no trouble on the left side, with all the trouble consisting mostly of gorse bush on the right side. This makes it difficult for the hacker who comes to Mecca with his horrible slice, as the gorse bush presents an unplayable lie every time. The contestants had a little trouble with the par 3 eighth because the prevailing wind was 20-25 mph, blowing hard right to left, making club selection difficult. Anything more than a six iron produced a shot that would end up off the green on the left producing a plethora of bogeys. By the end of the round the leaders had figured this out, hitting 8 irons into the 182-yard hole, producing mostly pars and an occasional birdie.

The par 4 17th hole (the Road Hole) presents the most significant challenge to the professional. The hole plays 467 yards and the tee shot has to cover the Old Course Hotel on the right side in order to have a reasonable chance of hitting the green. The Road Hole consistently plays to an average score over par during the tournament. Miguel Angel Jimenez hit the shot of the tournament when his second crossed the road and ended up snuggled against the wall.

Rather than take an unplayable penalty, Jimenez turned toward the crowd and bashed the ball against the wall backwards. The ball crossed the road and nestled toward the green stopping about nine feet from the hole. The crowd gave him a round of applause and he turned to them in elegant triumph. Unfortunately, the Road Hole won again, as his par putt slipped past the hole for a very entertaining bogey. Of course he birdied the 18th in revenge. Tiger Woods was almost in the same position on Saturday but had enough room to hit a very creative lob across the road to within a few feet, where he made par. The Old Lady would return the favor on Sunday as he double bogeyed the 14th. The 12th hole offered some resistance with a few balls in the gorse, including Paul Casey on championship Sunday. Mother Nature reared her head on a few days or the winner might have been 30 under par. As it was, Louis Oosthuizen, previously an unknown professional from South Africa, took advantage of the benign conditions on Friday morning and posted a 12 under par score that could not be overcome by the remaining participants, who had to play in the howling winds of the afternoon. It seems that tee times at St. Andrews might be a very significant factor in determining the outcome of the event. The 18th hole turned into a par 3 with numerous participants driving the 357-yard hole either onto the green and into the Valley of Sin, which actually served as a baptismal font for this Open. Grahame McDowell hit the stick and the ball ricocheted away almost further than the tee shot itself. Tom Lehmann had a tap in "eagle 2." There simply was no drama at the 18th for this Open Championship, as Oosthuizen was never seriously threatened by the field, so the onset of nerves and pressure could not penetrate the newly crowned champion. He was never tested by the field.

Still, the Old Girl looked handsome and worthy as the home of golf, as the place oozes class and utter history of Open championships gone by. It really doesn't matter how many under par the professionals can achieve; the Old Girl will survive the test of time.

A DAY WITH ARNOLD PALMER

One day in early May, 2004, I had an unexpected surprise at Pebble Beach Golf Links. I had been asked to play a round with a few executives and join them at Pebble Beach. I was told that Arnold Palmer would be there. Of course I graciously accepted and dutifully showed up at 11:15 a.m. for the noon tee time. I expected that I would be one of "n" players invited and that there would be multiple foursomes. Perhaps I would get to play a hole or two with Arnie. I had stayed at our Spyglass Hill home the previous evening and was really psyched to be playing Pebble. No matter how many times you play it, it's always a pleasure. I walked into the Pebble Beach Pro Shop to check in. One of the assistant professionals who was behind the counter said, "Mr. Palmer is waiting for you on the practice tee." I was pretty surprised to hear this and was escorted to the practice range. This wasn't the practice range on Stevenson Road where everybody who plays Pebble warms up…this was a different range that had been set up in the equestrian center just for today's event.

I got out of the van and Arnie came up to me and introduced himself and gave me the umbrella lapel pin which is the logo of the Arnold Palmer enterprise. That umbrella lapel pin has been stuck on my blazer ever since. He was charming and affable and to me ultimate surprise there was only one foursome going out this day. I was "blown away" and really psyched to play. We completed our warmup and proceeded back to the Pebble Beach starter's area. It was very weird day for May for Pebble Beach. The rainy season was over and we can always either look forward to bright blue skies or a rather chilly fog or gray sky that often envelopes the Monterrey Peninsula. Today was neither. I looked up and saw ominous-looking dark clouds. The air was musty and humid, which is highly unusual (almost never) for this time of year. As soon as we got back to the starter's area it actually began to thunder and you could seek streaks of lightning in the distance. This was virtually impossible, but I took it all in without much concern. We couldn't tee off in this kind of weather…thunder and lightning is the only weather condition that will keep me (and most people) off a golf course. It was very quiet and no one was around. There is a coffee shop right above the Pebble Beach shops called "The Gallery" where many Pebble Beach players get their breakfast or pregame meal before tackling the links. The four of us went up the stairs to hopefully wait out the thunderstorm. As I said, it was very quiet in the area and we walked in and sat down unceremoniously. Arnie had some coffee and we all started in on our various backgrounds and hoping that the weather would clear. At this point "The Gallery" began to fill up and then it started… "Look over there…it's Arnold Palmer," quipped one of the patrons. Very soon thereafter requests for autographs commenced, and then cameras began to appear out of nowhere. I enjoyed the scene immensely as Arnie graciously signed everything and posed for numerous pictures with children and adults alike. I was amazed that on a sleepy Thursday afternoon dampened by roars of thunderclaps where all these people had come from. I looked up and it was about 12:45 p.m.—forty-five minutes had passed our starting time, but it was about to happen. We went out the side door of "The Gallery" and down the steps leading to the first tee. As soon as we opened the door I was shocked to see that there must be about 500 people in the starter's area and lined up down the first fairway. Word of mouth had spread that Arnie was here and was about to begin a round of golf. Who were these other turkeys?? You could surmise the answer to that question from some of the new gallery. The first tee now resembled the first tee that would be evident at the AT&T Pro AM. It was a thick crowd.

I walked up to the tee with my driver and was confronted by

the former head professional at my club. He asked what in the world I was doing here playing Pebble Beach with Arnold Palmer. I told him it was all due to clean living and some good luck. We proceeded to the tee and my heart began to race. I was now going to have to perform in front of all these people and get the first tee shot off. I expected Arnie to lead us off and then the crowd would dissipate, not caring what we did, so I didn't feel much pressure. As I walked onto the tee Arnie flipped me a ball and told me to "lead the way."

Ouch--the pressure was on me, but I like this type of pressure and I took my driver and blasted the tee shot some 225 yards down the middle, which is exactly what is required on Hole #1.

The day was very special and Arnold joked, coached, and was the ultimate raconteur on the golf course. A photographer had been hired to memorialize the event, so we have the pictures to prove the day. The weather on the front nine was sunny and windy. We all played pretty well and I actually had a 38 on the front nine, besting Arnie by one stroke. The difference was on the famous par 3 7th hole of 107 yds. We had at least a 35 mph wind in our face and Arnie hit one to the right and nailed the cliffs as his ball found the grave called the Pacific Ocean. He hit a 4 iron and I did likewise but made the green, two putted, and left the premises with a par. My crowning achievement for the day was making par on the treacherous par 4 8th hole with a great drive to the chasm and a long iron to the green. Arnie played very well on the back nine, shooting one over par 37 to finish with a 76 besting my 78. Scoring didn't matter, as we all just enjoyed the day with his company, the stories and memories that will last a lifetime. Arnold Palmer is the consummate gentleman and has an inner passion for the game of golf that I have never experienced in a human being. There have been better players who have achieved more than Arnold on the golf course, such as Jack Nicklaus and Tiger Woods. Both Tiger and Jack may be the best competitors of all time that I have seen, but no one has the inner passion of competitiveness, love of the game, and the person that best embodies the principles of the game of golf that Arnold Palmer has. He is the "Champions' Champion" and there may never be anyone like him ever again.

Chapter 7
GOLF COURSES

NEW CLUBS AT THE KINGDOM

My friend called me and asked me if I needed a new set of golf clubs. I have a number of sets of golf clubs in many parts of the US and the UK so I never have to travel with them. I never travel with golf clubs unless I'm going on a golf vacation or playing somewhere really special like Augusta National. I have clubs in England, Cheshire, Connecticut, Scottsdale, Arizona, Maui, Hawaii, Long Beach, California and, of course, two extra sets (for guests) at our second home in Pebble Beach, California. In any event, I'm always up for a new experience. The Kingdom is the TaylorMade Golf Factory and Headquarters located in Carlsbad, California. At the Kingdom, professionals come to get their clubs made, swings analyzed, and lessons given by professional teachers. While I was there, the late Jim Flick gave me an impromptu lesson. We arrived at the Kingdom and proceeded to get our swings analyzed for club head speed. I was surprised with a relatively decent 102 mph with the driver, and a six-iron speed of 84 miles per hour, which the instructor stated was senior professional grade. After a bunch of photography, a CD is made out of all of this and it's off to the driving range for club fitting. After an hour of trying different things, we homed in on a set of irons, hybrids, and woods that really felt great. They were weighted based on the swing analysis that had been conducted earlier. The irons were lighter than my steel- shafted Top Flite tour irons (now in Austin) with which I had played for the last ten years. The material was tungsten, which was heavier than graphite but lighter than steel. The irons worked very well on the driving range, but took over a year to get used to on the golf course when I bought them for real play. It's now been three years and I still can't say that I'm really comfortable with these irons, but I am committed to them. The funny occurred when we moved to the putting studio to experiment with new Taylor Made putters. They asked you to bring your own putter so that you could compare your putter to the Taylor Made putter that they were about to sell you. I've been playing with an Odyssey "white hot" putter for the past number of years so I was highly doubtful that I was going to be changing putters, which is a traumatic experience for most golfers. The idea was to take six putts with your putter and then take six putts with the Taylor Made putter and see what happened. Well, inexplicably, I made all six putts from 18 ft in a row, to which the professional replied, "I don't think we're going to sell you a putter today." In fact, he did not...I could not part with the Odyssey and it remains in use to this day.

The day was very special and I parted with another new set of irons and woods, but this time they were customized and I could reorder at any time with the same specifications. Of course I managed to lose a wedge or two, so I've been able to reorder them from the Kingdom. I've also upgraded drivers to R-7 and then to R-9 using the same process. Now I have since added the R-11.

I didn't hit the R-11 reliably, but it did go 20-25 yards further for me. I had just bought my daughter Meredith a set of Titlelist clubs for Christmas and we went out one Sunday afternoon to try them out. I hit her driver--the women's Titlelist 910-D--extremely well so I had to try it. I demo'd the 910-D and it is safely in my bag today and it has been the best driver I've ever owned. I didn't miss a fairway the first seven rounds I played with it. It has changed my entire attitude and life toward the game.

THE HARDEST HOLES

The definition of the "hardest holes" in this book is those golf holes that were the hardest for me to play at my skill level. Today with the changes in equipment and the ball, some of these holes might not be viewed as difficult by the youngsters or professionals that smash a drive routinely 300 yards off the tee. I don't believe golf courses were ever meant or designed for such capability, although I still believe these holes are demanding to anyone.

NO. 4—ROYAL ST. GEORGE'S, ENGLAND

The fourth at Royal St. George's poses one of the most intimidating tee shots you could ever imagine. As you stand up on the tee, there is a huge bunker sculpted on the hillside about what seems to be 240 yards. For me it looked like 300 yards. You have to drive the ball over this bunker to reach the fairway. If you miss the fairway left, there is terrible knee-high rough, and missing the fairway to the right is equally horrible. You must clear the bunker and make the fairway, or your score could reach double digits.

It was a magical day in Sandwich, England. We had just completed a nice round at the Prince's Course the day before. This is the weekend where we started at the ghastly Royal Cinqueport venue which is chronicled in another part of this book, followed by Prince's on Sunday. The Prince's Course was nothing special and

I don't remember much about it except for the good weather and the friendly confines of the clubhouse and members--the exact opposite of what we experienced the day before at Royal Cinqueport. It was Monday and we didn't quite know what to expect at Royal St. George's, a majestic layout and a British Open venue. We were pretty excited about playing it but after our experience at Royal Cinqueport our guard was up as to how we would be greeted. We arrived to find virtually no one there, and the pro shop couldn't have been friendlier. When asked if there were restrictions as to which tees to play, the pro said, "Play from whatever tees you like…she's all yours. Thus we made our way out and played the first three holes well including the relatively easy Par 3 third. As we holed and moved to the adjacent tee just to our right—I looked and saw "the Bunker." I couldn't believe how big it was and how imposing it was and how far we would have to hit it to make the fairway. I remember it as one of the most intimidating tee shots I have experienced. My mind reverted back to Colin Montgomery being in that bunker during the British Open last held here. Brian moved to the tee and said "no use looking at it--we'll just have to clear it" and with his beautiful swing he did just that right over the bunker and into the fairway--a mere 250 yards away. I was pretty encouraged that if he could do it I could do also and off I went and lo and behold over the bunker and into the fairway about 10 yards behind Brian. We breached a huge sign of relief and managed to both get pars on the hole.

NO. 11-PASATIEMPO, SANTA CRUZ, CALIFORNIA

The eleventh at Pasatiempo is a par 4 of 425 yards that is uphill all the way. It's a very difficult hole, following the 10th hole at Pasatiempo, which in itself is 440 yards, so you get two murderous holes in a row. There is a ravine that cuts across the fairway from the left side of the hole all the way from 125 yards, cutting a swath across the left side of the fairway and snaking across all the way to the right side of the green. The fairway is generous, but you must hit the ball to the left side of the fairway in order to have a decent shot to the green. The hole continuously glides uphill, so club selection is tricky. If your tee shot isn't far enough, you have the option of laying up in front of the ravine, which will still leave a difficult 140-yard shot uphill, or hitting a shot that clears the ravine on the left side of the hole, which will leave you a 100-yard uphill shot to the green. There are no level lies in this fairway and starting at the ravine which must be traversed the second shot is daunting. There is no way to drive the ball over the bridge, as the carry would be over 325 yards. There are a lot of golf holes with looks such as this; however, the trouble doesn't end there. The green is rather large, with significant undulations, and anything hit short of the pin, particularly a pin placement at the beginning of the green, will roll off the green and end up some 25-30 yards from the green. Hitting this green in regulation is a great achievement and I've done it only a few times. The safe play is a drive in the fairway and then a long iron or even a fairway wood over the bridge to the middle or the left side on the other side of the bridge so that an approach shot for par can be attempted. The approach shot from the safe side over the bridge is approximately 80-100 yards. The greens at Pasatiempo are usually very fast, and this green is no exception. Subtle breaks at the hole for most pin placements are the norm. The green was so difficult to putt on that the green was redone in 2003 to remove some of the more severe undulations. In the past, any shot above the hole would be a sentence of bogey or double bogey since you just couldn't chip the ball onto the green from anywhere above the hole and have it stop anywhere on the green. I'll never forget one day when two of my playing partners airmailed the green with brilliant second shots and ended up taking 9 on the hole as their chips could not stop on the green.

No. 16-Cypress Point, Pebble Beach, California

The 16th at Cypress Point is a glorious golf hole. It's a par 3 that takes your breath away. The hole follows the beautiful par 3 15th hole that crosses a narrow inlet of the Pacific Ocean. The 16th is a lot different...you arrive at the tee box and there is nothing between you and the green 245 yards away but the roar of the Pacific Ocean. Depending on the wind, you'll either be hitting a driver or a 3 wood to this hole. For those that give up immediately and make it a par 4,there is a bail out area where you can hit the ball 175 yards and cross the Pacific Ocean. I have had many wonderful experiences on this hole. but one in particular stands out. I had been playing well one day and arrived at the 16th pretty pumped up. I selected a driver, since the wind was against us. I hit the ball very cleanly heading for the back right side of the green, but...oops... the ball hit and bounded all the way down to the beach below. It was disappointing, as we arrived to find the ball sitting up on the beach some 50 feet below. The only good news was that the tide was out and the ball was clearly visible. I shrugged my shoulders, clearly intending to take a drop and penalty stroke where the ball had cleared the green.

My caddie turned to me and said, "You've got this shot, go down there and hit it." I looked at him as if he had just landed on the planet Mars and told me that there was no way that I could get that shot on the green. In fact, I told him that I would probably hit the wall in front of me. He persisted, "Naw...we got this shot," so I proceeded to walk down to the beach and survey the situation. The caddie shouted instructions: "Open the club face and do not take any sand when you hit it. Just hit it right over my head!"

He stood there with more confidence in me than I could ever have in myself. I don't even remember what emotions went through me as I hit that shot. The ball lifted miraculously and went sailing over the caddie's head. I had no idea of what happened after that, as the shot was completely blind, standing on the beach in front of a wall. I was absolutely amazed to have hit the ball over the caddie's head. He kind of went slightly mad as he got very excited, as did my playing partners. I didn't see the result, since I had to walk some 25 yards from the beach. I looked up and exclaimed, "I couldn't do that again if I hit another 100 balls." I felt that without the concentration of hitting that shot, most attempts would have hit the wall in front of me since you had to get under the ball quickly to get it to lift. I climbed back up to the green to see where the shot ended up. I would have been very satisfied to have a 3- putt bogey after that experience. However, I was really excited to see the ball stopped about 8 inches from the hole, which I tapped in for an incredible par. Par from the beach was a new concept and something I doubt I could ever do again. Most professionals wouldn't be able to pull this off, either.

No. 17-The Road Hole at the Old Course at St. Andrews

The famous Road Hole at the Old Course of St. Andrews doesn't need much introduction as to its toughness. It's probably the hole with the highest stroke average for professionals in Europe. The hole is a treacherous 461-yard par 4, which requires a tee shot that seemingly has to go out of bounds to the right in order to reach the fairway. The first time I played this hole, the aim was over a rail line which hugged the right side of the hole to land the ball in the fairway. Today the rail line has been replaced with the St. Andrews Hotel, which is a wonderful place that houses most of St. Andrews' patrons. The hotel was built to accommodate those golfers from abroad who long to play the course and reminds me of the lodge at Pebble Beach. The interesting part is that the glass-enclosed sun room provides a wonderful view of the course and the hole. Look up and you'll see a myriad number of cracks and damage in the glass roof from errant tee shots that didn't make the fairway. Depending on wind conditions, always a factor at St. Andrews, the fairway is flanked on both sides by the annoying fescue grasses and weeds of links course rough. I don't think there are any gorse bushes on this hole. The approach shot to the green is long even for the professionals. For the amateur it will take a long iron or three wood, depending on the wind. Guarding the green on the left is the famous Road Hole bunker, which is an absolute horrible place and worse than Hell Bunker (14th hole). The Road Hole bunker is probably the most difficult shots in golf. The bunker is extremely steep, with an 85- degree angle to get out facing the green. The bunker is on the left side of the hole, probably no more than 15 feet, so it is almost impossible to get the ball close to the hole even if you can extricate yourself from the bunker. The sand in the Old Course bunkers is fluffy, so the club face must be wide open and you have to hit the ball very softly to get the elevation required to get the ball out of the bunker. Any attempt to finesse or shorten the swing cannot get sufficient elevation to get the ball out. Countless professionals have tried doing this, only to have their round ruined by leaving the ball in the bunker and making double, triple bogey, or worse. I've also seen a number of professionals actually putt their ball in the bunker to another spot in the bunker where they believe they can easily at least get the ball out of the bunker. On the right the "road" or path cuts a swath through the hole and all missed approach shots will end up across the road and near a retaining wall. Shots missed to the right will result in the player having to chip the ball onto to the green which is one of the most delicate shots in golf required. The results of these chip shots are either remarkable luck or worse with many good chips ending up 15-20 feet past the hole.

NO. 8—PEBBLE BEACH GOLF LINKS

The 8th hole at Pebble Beach is one of the most breathtaking holes in the world. There is absolutely nothing easy about this hole. From the back tee you have a blind tee shot to the left side of the stone marker (a good marker is the gate of a home literally ¼ mile away) to get the ball as close to the end of the fairway as you dare. Professionals usually hit 3 woods in order to carry the ball about 240 yards to the end of the fairway. The second shot is truly amazing, over a cliff that heads straight down to the beach of at least 200 feet. A long iron or hybrid club is demanded for a shot of 170-180 yards to an undulating green with multiple twists and turns. If the tee shot is not far enough or is off line to the left, there is no chance to get on the green, so a shot must be hit over the shortest part of the gorge, to where a pitch shot of anywhere from 50-75 yards is required. Trouble lurks everywhere as the second shot must be exacting and anything hit short is liable to end up in the rough that guards the green. This rough saved Tom Kite in the 1996 US Open, as without it his second shot would have been swallowed into the beach below. He was able to extricate himself from the deep rough and take a rather miraculous bogey. Club selection on this hole is critical and the drive must be in the middle of the fairway--or close--to have a clear second shot to the green. The green is guarded by treacherous bunkering and is one of the most difficult putting surfaces on the Monterrey Peninsula. Par is a great score for this hole no matter what the skill level.

No. 3-Pasatiempo Golf Club, Santa Cruz, California

Very few people have encountered a par 3 of this type. Pasatiempo is a private club that grants public access in the afternoons and was designed by Alistar McKenzie, who also designed Augusta National. The course is well-known to PGA tour professionals, and is one of their favorite layouts in the Bay Area. The course is located in Santa Cruz, California on the way to the Monterrey Peninsula. Unfortunately, the property is not large enough to lengthen the golf course and the tips measure a very tough 6,500 yds with a slope rating of 141. I have the good fortune of having a close friend as a member. The par 3 3rd hole is very difficult measuring 227 yards uphill so it really plays 240 yards. A par on this hole is something to be cherished. In order to reach the green, you will have to carry the ball the entire 227 yards in the air to reach the green, which is surrounded by horrific bunkers. The green is slightly elevated, and so a good shot that travels 200 yards may not run on to the green because of the elevation. The bunkers are horrific in the sense that there is no level lie in those bunkers. The green slopes toward the right, which makes any bunker shot delicate at best, as you extricate yourself from the bunker. The back pin placement is the worst in the sense that if you're chipping up to the green to that back pin, there is a mound on the green that has to be navigated to get the ball reasonably close to the hole. The club of choice is the driver as I try to fade the ball up the hill to the narrow receiving area that guards the green. Most times my ball doesn't make it up the hill and a delicate chip is required. If the pin is middle or front—a good chip will be rewarded and so a par is possible, but if not, big numbers will follow.

No. 12-Spanish Bay Golf Links, Pebble Beach, California

The Spanish Bay Golf Links inside the 17-mile drive of Pebble Beach is the course that gets the least respect of those owned by the Pebble Beach Company, given that the other two are Pebble Beach and Spyglass Hill. Surrounded by the Monterrey Peninsula Club and Cypress Point private clubs, Spanish Bay doesn't get a lot of respect. Yet it is one of my favorite courses because it is so playable, fun, and challenging all together. Good players will be hitting driver on only 6-7 holes, but that is what is so enticing about the course. I feel the 12th hole is an exception to the demeanor of the rest of the course. It is a mean, tough hole. It's a par 4 at 412 yards. If this hole were on another difficult course, it would just be another tough hole. At Spanish Bay, the hole is tougher in its relative sense to the other holes on the course which are less demanding. It makes the 12th hole harder than it actually is.

You must hit a very good tee shot of at least 240 yards if you want to make a par on this hole. The hole is straight away, but the fairway ends at about 290 yards and you must cross a baranca to approach a green that is slightly elevated to the end of the fairway. A straight tee shot is imperative, since going left off the tee provides a blind second shot which is almost impossible to cross the baranca and reach the green. A tee shot to the right will find high rough and require a 200-yard carry over the baranca which is a low-percentage shot. I have to lay up to the 125-yard mark if my tee shot doesn't measure up. The green is guarded on the right by some pretty terrible bunkers and the left yields rough and a tough chipping area mounded like Pinehurst No. 2. A par here is a very good score no matter how far you hit it.

No. 17—Cordevalle Golf Club, San Martin, California

Cordevalle is a private club in San Martin, California designed by Robert Trent Jones, Jr. The 17th at Cordevalle is a blistering 440-yard par 4 with a fairly narrow landing area for the tee shot, which is slightly downhill. Any tee shot missed to the right will find a grave down an embankment of at least 20 yards. I've seen an outstanding player hit a recovery shot from that embankment to the green from that position, which is one of the greatest shots I've ever seen hit by an amateur. Tee shots missed to the left will find some spinachy rough and a steep side hill lie. There is a bunker on the left about 290 yards from the tee which is an excellent marker as to where to land the tee shot. From 130 yards in lie a series of bunkers that guard the green. There are also a bunker and a tree guarding the right side of the green. The best play is a well-struck tee shot that should travel about 255 yards downhill, leaving a shot of 185 yards to carry the middle bunkers. Once again, par is a great score on this hole. There was a miraculous period of time (my caddie will attest) when I birdied this hole with a 3 wood second shot that ended up about 6 inches from the hole. I did this three times in a row. It was similar to when you make a hole-in-hole and then you seem to get close to another one very quickly for a few weeks and then nothing. The hole is gorgeous visually and the toughest hole on the course…when the wind is blowing against as it usually can…the hole will play close to 500 yards.

No. 18----Augusta National Golf Club

This hole probably wouldn't make the list of the hardest golf holes in the world, but it was a very difficult hole for me. I had the opportunity to play Augusta in 2003 for three consecutive days and I never "mastered" this hole. We've seen so many professionals screw up on this hole on TV that perhaps it deserves the "hardest" designation. Maybe a better term for this hole would "hardest hole in the world under the pressure of winning the Masters." I believe the professional golfer who has competed for the Masters at Augusta would endorse this designation. I certainly wasn't playing for much of anything other than a $5 Nassau, so I had no excuse to "screw up" on this hole. The hole is generally straight par 4 with a menacing bunker on the left side of the fairway. Kenny Perry knows this bunker, as it cost him the 2008 Masters title. The hole is uphill all the way, with bunkers that are strategically placed in front to guard the green, which is faster than you can imagine. My problem with this hole is that my educated "fade" drive kept landing in the pine straw to the right of the fairway and so I never really had an approach shot to the green for any of the three days I played there. It was the only hole I played consistently poorly, with three double bogeys over the three rounds played.

HARDEST GOLF COURSE

HOLE 1—SPYGLASS HILL GOLF COURSE

Spyglass Hill is the terror of the Monterrey Peninsula. It is revered by all who play it and many players prefer the course to its sister one mile away–Pebble Beach Golf Links. Actually holes 1-4 are probably the toughest stretch of four consecutive holes you will find in the game of golf. The first hole is a par 5 of some 555 yards where a drive of 250 yards in the center will give you the opportunity to go over the 50 yards of bunkers that guard the front of the green. The tee shot must be center right—large trees on both sides define the width but you will not find a level lie after your drive. You then choose to hit a second shot as far as you can toward those bunkers that guard the green. A well-hit drive and accurate wood shot might give you an approach shot of 140-150 yards over those bunkers to a very large green that is vertically large but horizontally narrow. Fly the green and you reach the dreaded phenomenon called the "ice plant."

I once played with a business associate who stepped up to the tee and blasted a 280-yard drive perfectly right center in the middle of the fairway. This was after I had described how difficult the hole was. He looked at me as if I had no idea of what I was talking about it. This hole was easy! I congratulated him and asked him what club he was going to hit to have an easy approach shot. He said confidently, "I'm not laying up," and took out his three-wood. I advised him against it, because it demanded an almost perfect shot that would have to be accurate and land softly on the green. Of course he proceeded to push the shot into the right into the ice plants. The ice plant is a strange plant that is quite native to links courses and is prevalent on the Monterrey Peninsula. It's is a lush green bush that looks a bit like ivy but is a thicker version. Balls hit into ice plants usually are sitting up and look very simple to extricate yourself from this problem. Here is the ball sitting up and it looks like you'll be able to get the clubface on the ball easily. Well most of the time it doesn't happen. The ice plant devours the golf ball when hit and the ball usually stays in the ice plant or moves a few feet. My friend thought the ice plant was no problem and he ended up taking a 9 on the par 5 hole needing 3 shots to extricate from the ice plant. I believe the way to play the hole is to play it for three shots onto the green. Your second shot should be layup to the bunkers that guard the hole giving you a shot to the large green of between 110-130 yards, which is my way of trying to make par or birdie. There are outrageous numbers to be made on Spyglass No. 1 and it hurts to start a round that way.

Nos. 1 through 4 at Spyglass Hill Golf Course

I have never seen a more treacherous beginning to a round of golf that at Spyglass Hill than holes 1 through 4. The holes are very different and very difficult, particularly for the high handicapper or those players who are not familiar with the course. Sometimes it is brutal taking a customer and trying to entertain him/her at Spyglass. I've seen people almost walk off the course after playing the first four holes. I have just described the first hole and while the next three holes wouldn't make "my hardest" list…the first four holes taken as a whole are the most difficult first four holes I have ever encountered in the game of golf. When the wind is blowing hard, these holes can be impossible. The second hole is a short par 4 with an elevated green. Bunkers, ice plants, and other types of gunk shape the hole, so missing the green short with your approach shot will result in a big number. The tee shot requires an iron or hybrid club to hit 175 yards or so, which must be in the fairway to avoid all the rest of the trouble that the hole offers. The approach shot is anywhere between a 6 to an 8 iron that must make it to the green to avoid all the trouble. The green is very small, and going over the green will make for a difficult chip shot which is virtually impossible to get close. The 3rd hole is probably the most scenic at Spyglass, as you face the Pacific Ocean—a par 3 which is only 150 yards downhill—a steep downhill. Club selection is paramount and is also totally dependent on whether the wind is blowing. The prevailing wind is a cross wind, usually right to left, but if it turns against into your face—you could end up hitting 4 iron to this green. It's all or nothing on this hole since the hole is carved out of beach, ice plant, and all sorts of bad vegetation, so missing the green is not an option. There is a bunker in the front of the green that is blind to the tee shot, but it will catch anything short. Any tee shot over the green will be welcomed by ice plant. If you have played the first two holes badly—your confidence could be shattered by this hole. You will be upset if you don't get a par on this hole but if you miss the green you could easily make 6 or 7. The final dose of torture is the 4th hole, which is a short par 4 of 350 yards which is a dogleg to the left. You must traverse 175 yards of beach sand and ice plant to reach the fairway. If you hook the ball to the left you will need a carry of 215 yards to reach the fairway. If you hit the ball straight but too far through the fairway—it will find the iceplant. The play is usually a 3 wood to the fairway. If you succeed at reaching the fairway, the second shot is a short iron to a very small green that is actually shaped like a narrow rectangle. There is a hideous bunker in the back of the green just in case you are a tad long with your approach shot. I made a 13 on this hole once by hitting my tee shot through the green and landing in ice plant. Believing that I could easily hit the shot out of the ice plant, I proceeded to take 4 whacks out of the ice plant and advanced the ball a total of 5 yards. Hitting 6 from the fairway, I managed to put the ball into the back bunker. I then thought I hit a great bunker shot, but it came out and spun backward right back into the bunker. I then missed another bunker shot and five- putted for a 13—you had to be there! Despite this disaster, I've also had a number of birdies of this hole. I choose to remember the birdies and try to forget the 13 when I play the hole—but as we all know—you can't forget the 13.

I believe the first four holes at Spyglass are the toughest group of holes that I have ever played, considering them as a group of holes. If you get off to a bad start on these holes—the rest of Spyglass will eat you alive. It is very important to get through these holes with your mind and confidence intact.

HOLE 2—OLYMPIC CLUB-LAKE COURSE

The opening hole at the Lake Course at the Olympic Golf Club in San Francisco is actually an easy Par 5 birdie hole, but it all ends there. The second hole is the beginning of significant treachery. This hole begins a pretty difficult stretch of holes at the Olympic Club, which isn't seen very much on TV. The hole is a long par 4, which gradually moves up the hill, playing over 450 yards. The fairway is completely sloped, with no level lies, so if you hit the fairway, the second shot is difficult—all uphill into a sloping green surrounded by bunkers. The approach shot from the fairway is daunting, since you need to add at least one club to the yardage on a fairway that is sloped significantly to the left. Missing the fairway on the right side will make it virtually impossible to get to the green and missing left will cause the shot lose yardage and roll down the hill. The green is surrounded by bunkers which generally characterizes Olympic. After getting your confidence up on the easy 1st hole, you are jolted into reality on this hole where double bogeys will result from any errant shot.

HOLE 3- PASATIEMPO GOLF CLUB

I described this hole in the preceding section, but I can't say enough about how hard it is. The back tee plays at 227 yards, which requires a tee shot of at least 250 yards to make the green, as the tee is way below the hole, making the tee uphill. The bunkering on this hole is treacherous, as short shots will be caught, and potentially shots that are hit straight but short may end up in the sand. The green is tiered and slopes a bit toward the ocean. When the greens are cut to tournament condition, this is one of the most difficult greens to putt on the golf course--or any golf course. Par is an out-standing score here even for the low-handicap player.

HOLE 4 ROYAL ST. GEORGE'S

The fourth at Royal St. George's poses one of the most intimidating tee shots you can ever imagine. As you stand up on the tee, there is a huge bunker sculpted on the hillside about what seems to be 240 yards away. For me, it looked like 300 yards. You must drive the ball over this bunker to reach the fairway. If you miss the fairway to the left, there is terrible knee-high rough, and missing to the right is equally horrible. You clear the bunker and make the fairway or you can end up with a double-digit score on the hole.

The day we played there it was a magical day in Sandwich, England. We had just completed a nice round at the Prince's Course the day before. This was the weekend where we started at the ghastly Royal Cinqueport venue followed by Prince's on Sunday. The Cinqueport story is a sad and chronicled elsewhere in this work. The Prince's Course was nothing special and I don't remember very much about except for the great weather and the friendly confines of the clubhouse and members--exactly the opposite of what we experienced the day before at Royal Cinqueport. It was a Monday and we didn't know what to expect at Royal St. George's, a majestic layout and a British Open venue course. We were pretty excited about playing, but after Cinqueport, our guard was up as to how we would be received. We arrived to find virtually no one there and the pro shop couldn't have been friendlier.

When asked if there were restrictions as to which tees could be played, the pro said, "Play from whatever tees you like…she's all yours. Thus we made our way out and played the first three holes well including the easy par 3 third. As we holed out and moved to the adjacent tee box just to our right—I glanced and saw "the Bunker." I couldn't believe how big it was and how imposing it was and how far we would have to hit it to make the fairway. I remember it as one of the most intimidating tee shots I have ever experienced. My mind reverted back to Colin Montgomery being in the bunker during the British Open. Brian moved to the tee and said, "No use looking at it--we'll just have to clear it," and with his beautiful swing he did just that and nailed his drive over the bunker and into the fairway…a mere 250 yards away. I was pretty encouraged that if he could do it, I could do it also, and so I blasted it over the bunker as well about 5 yards behind Brian. We each breathed a sigh of relief and managed pars on the hole.

HOLE 5—CORDEVALLE GOLF CLUB

The fifth hole at Cordevalle measures 440 yards from the men's back tee and plays into a prevailing wind that is usually in your face, which makes it play closer to 500 yards. While the fairway is reasonably generous, there is a treacherous bunker on the right that can grab many a tee shot. For a long hitter, it takes a drive of 280 yards or more to clear that bunker. The play is to the left center of the fairway, where a long shot of 200 yards or more is usually required. The green is immense, so the positioning of the approach shot is critical, as the green is the size of a green at the Old Course at St. Andrews. Although the green is large, the right approach requires a shot over a menacing bunker. The hole is fairly deceptively uphill which makes club selection difficult for the uninitiated. The hole also presents significant rough and a slightly errant tee shot will take 30-50 yards off the tee shot. On most days, this is really a par 5 for most of us.

HOLE 6—STANFORD UNIVERSITY GOLF COURSE-
PALO ALTO, CALIFORNIA

The Stanford University Golf Course is a very respected venue in the San Francisco Bay Area. It has many interesting holes particularly on the back nine but, for me, the No. 1 handicap sixth hole is a beast. The hole measures 408 yards from the back tees and demands an accurate tee shot. The fairway slants a bit toward the right, where there is rough and trees, where you cannot be off the tee. The second shot must carry a gorge that is about 50 yards from the green and you must be in the middle of the fairway or the left side of the fairway to have a good angle to the green. Wind can be a factor if it is blowing, since the prevailing wind is usually against the player, increasing the difficulty of the second shot. It takes two very good shots to negotiate all of this and put one in a position to make par or better. The hole is difficult for those players who can't hit the drive 250 yards or more.

Hole 7—Spanish Bay Golf Links

This is a very interesting hole for all levels of players. The hole marks the beginning of a return toward the Pacific Ocean and is shaped by native grasses and reeds on the left side of the fairway, where any wayward shot will find its grave. There is a bit of room on the right, but missing right will make the hole longer and more treacherous. The hole is 375 yards and there is a natural hazard (about 25 yards long) that the second shot must carry. A long hitter may have to lay up the tee shot with a three wood to about 130 yards from the green, which will be just short of the hazard. Most players will have second shots to the green of around 175-180 yards into a prevailing wind that is normally in your face. The green is very large (almost St. Andrews-like) and guarded by an enormous bunker on the right of the green. The left side of the green can't be used, as balls hit to the left or even slightly over the green will end up in the fairway hazard that continues all the way to the green. The marshland (wetlands) meanders through the left side of the green to form a natural water hazard for the par 3 8th hole at Spanish Bay. Wind is always an issue on this hole and this is why it is a "hard hole." Second shots are usually hybrid clubs or longer.

HOLE 8: PEBBLE BEACH GOLF LINKS

The 8th hole at Pebble Beach is one of the most breathtaking holes in the world. There is absolutely nothing easy about this hole. From the back tee, you have a blind tee shot to the left side of the stone marker to get the ball as close to the end of the fairway as you dare. Professionals usually hit 3 woods or today probably hybrid clubs in order to carry the ball about 240 yards to the end of the fairway. The second shot is over the cliffs that heads straight down to the beach of at least 200 feet. A long iron or hybrid club is demanded for a shot of 170-180 yards to an undulating green with multiple twists and turns. Trouble lurks everywhere, as the second shot must be exacting, and anything hit short is liable to end up in the rough that guards the green. Shots from the cliff that are wayward to the left bring a whole series of bunkers into play. The difficulty with being on the left side of the hole is that you cannot stop a chip shot on the green, as the green will push the ball toward the ocean. You won't see many up-and-downs from the left side of this fairway. You are actually better off in the bunkers. Putting on this green is very difficult due to the undulations combined with the usual wind conditions, which also plays havoc with the speed and line of the putts.

HOLE 8—SPYGLASS HILL GOLF CLUB

Although I have discussed No. 8 at Pebble Beach as very difficult, the eighth at Spyglass presents quite a challenge. It is the No. 1 handicap hole on a very difficult golf course. The hole is a par 4, measuring about 380-400 yards, all uphill. The hole swirls around to almost a dogleg left as the green is not visible from the tee. Trees hug the left side of the hole from tee to green and you absolutely cannot be playing from the left side of the hole. Even if you hit the fairway on the left, you will have a very difficult second shot, which will demand almost a complete hook. The approach for the tee ball must be the center to center/right of the fairway. An errant tee shot to the right will considerably lengthen the hole, and the slope of the hill will be quite steep from that angle. The problem with this hole and that club selection is difficult. Any shot short of the hole will be difficult to get up and down to make par. An approach shot from the right-hand side of the fairway has to clear a series of menacing bunkers on the right guarding the green. The green is very large and undulating. I believe the green is one of the largest --if not the largest--greens on the Spyglass course. Three putts here will be frequent.

HOLE 9—PEBBLE BEACH GOLF LINKS

Pebble's No. 9 is another "links" hole measuring 450 yards. It's a beautiful hole, requiring length off the tee and a terrific second shot to reach the green. The Pacific Ocean is on the right and moves right on up to the hole, so any shot hit to the right will end up on the beach. Errant shots to the left will be punished with a barrage of bad things including bunkers, high grass, boulders, and other nasty stuff. The green is rather small, with the usual break toward the ocean. If there is significant wind, the prevailing wind is "in your face." It will be next to impossible to reach this green in regulation. Touring professionals and long hitters can't negotiate getting on the green in regulation when the wind is up. At the 2014 AT&T Pro-AM, I watched Phil Mickelsen hit two monstrous woods on the 9th only to end up 40 yards short of the green. Professionals are happy to make par here and move on, but many of them do not.

HOLES 9 AND 10—YALE UNIVERSITY GOLF CLUB, NEW HAVEN, CONNECTICUT

The difficulty at Yale peaks on these two holes. The 9th hole is a par 3 measuring 190 yards from the regular tee and 212 yards from the championship tee. The tee shot must carry the lake at about 180 yards with significant trouble if the green is missed. There is also trouble even if you land the ball on the green. The green is a triple-decker with a large swale that will catch shots that find the green, but make it into the swale. It's almost having a "valley of sin" on the green. If the pin is on the first tier, you will be putting uphill with a severe right-to-left break. If you're putting to the 3rd tier back pin, the green slopes severely from right to left, making it nearly impossible to get to the hole for a two-putt par. Bogey is a good score, but there will be plenty of "others."

Just walking up to the 10th hole is a chore in itself. You trudge up a path replete with medieval rocks, dirt, and other natural objects. Watch your ankles and beware of the bugs. The hole is 396 yards par 4 completely uphill. The tee shot is completely blind as you face a large knoll that you must carry-the knoll is only 50 yards from the teebox but it must be at 10 degrees as you cross it. The shot is intimidating. Depending where the tee shot lands, you will have an iron shot that must carry another bluff to get onto the green. If you execute a terrific drive of 240-250 yards, you will be rewarded by landing in a swale with the next shot completely blind due to the uphill. A well-placed bunker below the green will catch an accurate but short shot. The green is two-tiered, so you must stay below the hole. This course, like many university courses, is a real gem and could host a professional USGA event except for the fact that it could never accommodate spectators for that type of tournament.

HOLE 11—PASATIEMPO GOLF CLUB

This is another great designed hole by designer Alistar Mackenzie. The hole is a long par 4 of 420 yards which plays more like 460 yards because it is entirely uphill and a slight dogleg to the left. The hole demands a long tee shot to the end of the fairway of some 275 yards uphill which will leave an iron shot of 145 yards to the hole. Anything short of 275 yards presents difficulties for the player, since there are no level lies in the fairway and the baranca crosses the fairway and continues all the way guarding the green on the right. Any shot to the right must be well-struck or it will not carry the gorge, and the prevailing wind can blow the ball into the gorge. If the tee shot is less than 210 yards, it usually makes sense to lay up to the end of the fairway, which would leave an approach of about 135 yards. The other approach is to simply hit a fairway wood over the bridge and focus on the next shot, which would be between 70-90 yards. The green is large and very difficult to putt. The green was so difficult that a few years ago, the club redid the green to remove some of the undulation, but unfortunately I don't see much change between old and new. The green is extremely tiered and is slightly elevated, so pitch shots must carry the front part of the green on the green or else the ball will roll off the green potentially 40 yards into the fairway. There are many ways to play the hole but for me par it is a 2 out of 10 proposition—mostly bogies and sometimes others. You can make a very big number of this hole. Pasatiempo hosts a number of Western collegiate championships and tournaments and I'm sure that many good amateur players have had trouble with this hole.

HOLE 12—SPANISH BAY GOLF LINKS

Spanish Bay is the most playable of the Pebble Beach Company golf courses. I find it a pleasure to play it because you have to think your way around the course and it is not imperative to hit the golf ball 300 yards with a driver. I'll bet most professionals would use a driver on only 1 or 2 of the holes. One of those holes would be the 12th, a long par 4 of 420 yards which demands a long and accurate tee shot. The fairway runs out at about 300 yards to a baranca that must be crossed to an elevated green with steep bunkers on the right to a very large green, so the approach shot to the green must be precise, and predominantly in front of the hole. A drive of 240 yards may require a layup shot, since the landing area narrows the farther you drive the ball. I believe that this is the strongest hole on what is otherwise a fun and very playable golf course.

HOLE 13- KIAWAH ISLAND, SOUTH CAROLINA

The 13th hole is a terrific par 4 measuring 371 yards as water is in play from tee to green on the right side of the hole. There is a waste area that runs all the way to the hole to the green on the left. The green is guarded by the water on the right, waste area on the left, with five bunkers in between. The tendency is to play away from the water on the approach shot, which can lead to a number of bunker shots or shots out of the waste area. Another bunker is appropriately placed on the left side of the fairway, which can easily catch a tee shot that seeks to avoid the water on the right.

HOLE 13—CORDEVALLE GOLF CLUB

As a member of Cordevalle I am quite prejudiced positively about the golf course. The 13th is a terrific par 4 which plays at 425 yards from the back tees. The tee shot must carry 210 yards, which is slightly uphill. The fairway at the beginning is a narrow funnel with a hazard on the left. The right side of the fairway is scrub brush and what seems to be equivalent to a grassy fairway bunker with lies that range from promising to impossible. The drive has to be long and absolutely accurate, since there isn't a lot of fairway to work with. The width of the fairway from that grassy bunker to the hazard on the left can't be more than 15 yards. Therefore, the tee shot must clear this area, as the fairway opens wide once this point has been navigated. The green is rather large, but is very undulating, and shots hit short of it will leave difficult pitches to the hole. The middle pin position is usually on a mound, and shots landing short will roll off the green. The most difficult pin position is back right where the green slopes seriously from back to front. It is virtually impossible to make par if you fly the green with that pin position, as the rough is a tangled wad of spinach, which will leave very little control for a pitch to the back pin. The green is well-bunkered on both sides of the hole. Sand save percentages on this hole are low due to the undulations in the green and difficulty of pitching it close. To get a par here, a green hit in regulation is usually required.

HOLE 14—PEBBLE BEACH GOLF LINKS

The par 5 14th at Pebble Beach has become a very difficult hole. It has also become one of the most difficult holes on the PGA Tour and played as the hardest hole in the 2010 US Open. It takes 3 terrific shots to reach the green. I used to think that this was a fairly easy hole, but at some point in time, the 14th was lengthened to 565 yards. There is no trouble to begin with, as you can hit a tee shot into a very generous fairway and follow it up with another fairway wood. The problem for me is that my third shot to the green ranges from 165-180 yards and it used to be 140 yards before the hole was lengthened. Now, I'm hitting a 5 iron or a hybrid club into the green instead of an 8 or 9 iron. The green also appears to be different (in the last several years) as it is crowned with the huge bunker in front of the green. The bunker was always there to guard the pin position, which is usually just behind it. The problem with landing the ball in the bunker is that the pin is usually sitting on top of the crown on the green, and anything hit past the pin will end up off the green similar to an experience at Pinehurst No. 2—a pitchback where it is almost impossible to get the ball close to the hole. Just ask the professionals--they continued to try and fly the ball into the pin, only to see it fly past and end up over the green for a terrible pitch back to the hole. I am now content to usually lay up with my third shot to 50 yards and try to hit a lob wedge to the green and give me a putt for par.

HOLE 15—PINE VALLEY COUNTRY CLUB

Pine Valley could probably occupy most of the hardest holes on this layout, but I selected one of the most difficult-the 15th. The hole measures 591 yards as a par 5 (should be a par 6). It's a pretty narrow fairway for a long par 5, as the tee shot needs to be played down the right side of the fairway. The hole plays into the prevailing wind, increasing the yardage to over 600 yards. Visually, you start with a tee shot that looks daunting, as you have to cross the water, which is only 100 yards but visually appears to be 200 yards. After clearing the water, you continue a long uphill trek. Problems abound--shots hit center of right of the fairway will end up in terrible rough. Shots to the left will end up even worse into areas that are inhospitable at best. Not to mention, there are 20 bunkers on the whole, most of which you can't see until your perfect approach shot lands in one of them. Bunkers abound at Pine Valley and there are no rakes in these bunkers, management simply asks you to clean up after you extricate yourself to maintain pace of play. If everybody had to rake a bunker in Pine Valley, rounds would be in the seven-hour range. The green is diabolical. The green has a false front and shots need to carry at least 30 feet onto the green to hold or end up in New Jersey's version of the Valley of Sin.

It was easy to select Pine Valley, since the course is probably the most difficult golf course in the world, so one of these holes had to be selected.

My experiences haven't really uncovered very difficult 15th holes. The 15th hole in my experience seems to be a respite between very difficult 14th and 16th holes in my experience. Examples that come to mind are at Pebble Beach, Spyglass Hill, Cordevalle, and a host of others.

I also selected San Jose Country Club's 15th, which is a mirror image of their 12th hole, which I find almost impossible to make par. The 15th hole measures only 360 yards from the back tee, and the tee shot is straightforward, with a generous fairway. The second shot is the key shot, since the hole is severely inclined where it adds at least one if not two clubs to shot selection. Due to the uphill nature of the hole, tee shots will usually stop where hit, irrespective of the conditions. The second shot has to be below the pin, as the green is severely sloped back to front, with severe undulations depending on the pin position. There are some diabolical pin placements on this hole. Shots to the green that land past the pin will require some serious skill to two-putt this green. During the summer months, greens at San Jose will be extremely fast and this hole is one of the fastest: 3- or 4- putting is not uncommon. Roger Maltbie, the regular commentator at major golf events for NBC Sports, is a member of San Jose Country Club and grew up there where he learned to play. He had some reasonably good success on the PGA Tour and does a terrific job on golf telecasts and understands the details of what the professional is trying to accomplish under competitive conditions.

HOLE 16—SPYGLASS HILL GOLF CLUB

The 16th hole at Spyglass is a long difficult par 4 dogleg to the right, which demands two very good shots to reach the green. The hole is 435 yards and the tee shot must be in the middle or right hand side of the fairway to have any chance of going for the green. There is a huge cypress tree that marks the dogleg, so a miss to the right is either a lost ball or a lost shot, as the tree and other scrub brush will block the shot to the green. The second shot is usually a long iron or hybrid club to the green. While the landing area for the tee shot is generous, the fairway narrows significantly. The second shot is usually 160-175 yards and requires accuracy, as the green is surrounded by bunkers and flying the green will leave a difficult chip coming back. The green is well-bunkered, with an undulated green. This green doesn't seem to get as much sun as the rest of the course and may putt differently from the others.

HOLE 17---KIAWAH ISLAND, SOUTH CAROLINA

The 17th at Kiawah is an infamous par 3, measuring 160-197 depending on the tees you're playing. The hole usually plays at least one or possibly two clubs longer due to the prevailing wind. The wind can play tricks on you on this hole, as it seems to change direction from what you believe on the tee to what is happening on the green. It's a similar experience to playing the 12th at Augusta, where the swirling winds have often punished the professional who misjudged club selection. Club selection on this hole is also difficult. I chose a six iron from about 160 yards and absolutely flushed it--right into the back bunker of the left. I was very disappointed, since I hit the ball perfectly, but failed to judge the wind properly, as a seven iron would have made the green. The fear of being short and landing into the water will influence club selection. I proceeded to make bogey from that back bunker. The hole is a lot more intimidating from the back tee where club selection is even more critical. This hole was Mark Calcavecchia's "Waterloo" during the 1996 Ryder Cup, dunking his tee shot into the water to lose his match.

HOLE 18— RIVIERA COUNTRY CLUB

The 18th hole at Riviera Country Club in Pacific Palisades, California is a par 4 of 451 yards from the back tees and 412 yards from the member tees. I believe this hole is a terrific match of beauty and difficulty, as the tee shot is uphill and must carry at least 220 yards to get to a level lie position. The hole slightly veers to the right and everything actually moves to the right. The second shot is going to a medium iron for the professional and a long iron or wood for the typical player. You can bail out to the left and be greeted with Riviera's famous Kikuyu rough. The second shot from the right side of the fairway must avoid the trees on the right, and a miss right will leave a very difficult uphill chip shot. The hole is also guarded on the right side by bunkers, so the approach shot is a demanding one. The green is rather large and getting the ball to a decent position on the green is paramount if you want to avoid the dreaded 3 putt. The current home of the Northern Trust Open on the PGA Tour and a former US Open venue, many an important shot and putt has been played here.

MOST ENJOYABLE GOLF HOLES

I have selected the holes I have enjoyed the most, and therefore have created the most enjoyable golf course by hole from all of the courses I have played. These are holes that are visually beautiful and also afford me the opportunity to make par or better.

HOLE 1: SPANISH BAY GOLF LINKS

No. 1 at Spanish Bay on the Monterrey Peninsula is a gorgeous golf hole, with generous views of the Pacific Ocean as you tee off. It reminds me of the Old Course at St. Andrews, with very wide fairways and very level lies. The hole measures 505 yards. It is difficult if you want to reach the green with two shots, since the fairway narrows and has a lot of potential trouble from 80 yards into the green. The best play is a medium iron for the second shot leaving about 90-100 yards for the approach to the green. The green is deep, but not wide, and an approach that lands to the right will end up in a swale. Putting from this position will make it difficult to make par. The green is not easy and the best place for the approach shot is below the hole. This can be a brutal hole for the very high handicapper.

HOLE 2: PORT MARNOCK, DUBLIN IRELAND

I have had the good fortune of having to visit Dublin for the past five years, and will continue to go there for business. Port Marnock is always on the list of places to play. The course is very enjoyable and open generously with two par 4's. The second hole is a straightforward par 4 of 350 yards. A good tee shot in the middle of the fairway will give you no more than a wedge or 9 iron into the green. The green slopes front to back so you have to hit it short to bounce it on the green. This hole is a fond memory for me as I recorded an eagle 2 from 105 yards out a few years ago.

HOLE 3: PEBBLE BEACH GOLF COURSE, PEBBLE BEACH, CALIFORNIA

The third hole at Pebble is a short par 4 that can be played a number of different ways. New tee boxes were installed a few years ago, so the hole can play anywhere from 290 yards to the new professional tee of 365 yards. The aggressive play from the tee is to take driver and aim for the left side of the fairway, which requires a pretty accurate shot of at least 225 yards. From there, it is only a wedge shot to a small green and the left side is the best angle. There used to be a large cypress tree guarding the left side of this hole but it was removed about 10 ten years ago and was replanted on the 18th hole to replace the previous cypress tree that died there. A more conservative play would be a tee shot in the middle of the fairway with a 3 wood or a hybrid club, leaving a second shot of 150 yards to the green. A drive hit too far could catch one of the two fairway bunkers that guard the left side of the hole and are definitely in play. The best approach into the hole is a shot below the hole that will run on a bit, as the hole breaks toward the ocean. Shots that miss this green may result in some difficult pitches and big numbers. Tiger Woods made an 8 on this hole during his spectacular US Open victory at Pebble in 2000. The hole is visually gorgeous and the green adjoins the tee box at the 17th hole.

HOLE 4: TURNBERRY SCOTLAND-AILSA COURSE

The fourth at Turnberry is a par 3 called "Woe-Be-Tide." The hole plays between 155-165 yards and the prevailing wind runs from the left which is the Firth of Clyde to the right. If the wind is howling (it usually is), you have to aim courageously to put the ball into the waters of the Firth, as the wind will blow it back onto the green. Any well-struck shot aimed at the green will end up in the high grass on the right side of the green…or worse. It takes courage to aim the ball into the Firth, but if you aim for the green, it is likely that you will miss the green to the right.

HOLE 5: MONTERREY PENINSULA SHORE COURSE

The 5th on the Shore Course at Monterrey Peninsula is short par 4 of 310 yards. Trouble lurks everywhere, as the right side is sand virtually from tee to green. If you miss farther to the right, high native grasses will extol at least one shot. The fairway is generous, but not that wide, so shots pulled to the left will find trouble, and no way of getting to the green. The green is well bunkered on the left and the native hazard on the right continues all the way through the green, so a shot that goes over the green will be in deep trouble. A well- placed hybrid or 3 wood to the fairway will leave a short iron to the green.

HOLE 6: PEBBLE BEACH GOLF LINKS

The sixth hole at Pebble is a Par 5 of 510 yards. The tee shot is downhill with the fairway sloping to the right where it can become the Pacific Open. Menacing bunkers guard the left side of the fairway and will be cost you at least one shot if you enter one of these three bunkers. The second shot is the key shot on the hole, since a large uphill mound must be carried for a short approach to the green. Any shot that doesn't carry the mound can extract significant pain, as the ball will be in terrible rough and the shot to the green will be blind. Therefore this hole is defined by the first two shots. Carrying the mound in two shots will allow for an approach shot to the green of less than 130 yards with a few traps on the left, which should be avoidable. My favorite story on this hole is Tiger Woods' drive on this hole during the 2000 US Open where he drove the ball to the base of the mound some 360 yards off the tee.

HOLE 7: PEBBLE BEACH GOLF LINKS

The famous 107-yard par 3 at Pebble Beach demands only a lob wedge or a pitching wedge unless the wind is up. It's been a long time since I've seen significant wind in your face on this hole, but it can happen. All that is required is a simple "flip" of the wedge hit relatively cleanly to make the green and be in a birdie position. Any errant shot on this hole is usually fodder for the Pacific Ocean. I've hit a 4 iron on this hole playing with Arnold Palmer in a howling wind. The hole is intimidating, as it's surrounded by bunkers and the rocks that lead to the Pacific Ocean. For the decent player, this hole should be an easy par most of the time.

HOLE 8-CORDEVALLE GOLF CLUB

The eighth hole at Cordevalle is a par 4 measuring from 285 yards to 350 yards. A drive in the fairway will leave a short iron to the green, which makes the hole an easy par. In the Frys.com open, the course is inverted at Cordevalle and the 8th hole becomes the 17th hole. The professionals actually play the hole as if it were a par 3, and many birdies are recorded during the tournament. The hole is set up for significant drama in a close tournament, with the pros aiming to drive the green. From the short tee box, the pros can drive the green with a 3 wood. The interesting aspects to the hole are that water guards the hole from tee to green on the right and will catch any wayward shot. The fairway is relatively narrow with high rough on the left. The green is heavily guarded by bunkers and thick grass surrounds the green. The green is marked by a significant slope from back to front which can act as a backboard. If you miss the green long, the amateur will have an almost impossible shot of chipping the ball and stopping it anywhere close to the hole. I marvel at the professionals who are able to stop the ball most of the time within 6-8 feet after they have driven the hole through the green. Some of the professionals lay up to 100 yards and use their short game skills. Rocco Mediate holed out for eagle from 111 yards on the hole on the way to winning the tournament in 2009.

One year during our club championship in alternate shot competition, the first player knocked his drive into the water on the right. His partner then had to hit the next tee shot, since the tee was the closest relief. The partner drove the green about 285 yards but had a 50-foot putt for par. The partner that hit the tee ball in the water now had to hit this putt. The putt was miraculously holed and the two of them went on to win the championship. A highly unlikely outcome!

HOLE 9--BOULDER RIDGE COUNTRY CLUB, SAN JOSE, CALIFORNIA

Boulder's 9th hole is a par 4 of 360 yards and has the widest fairway on the course--and one of the widest I've ever seen anywhere.

The hole is deceptively uphill and plays longer than its yardage, so you must add a club for the approach shot. The long driver will not have a problem with this hole, as the green will be receptive to the short iron. The shorter hitter has to be left to avoid having to carry the bunkers with a long iron. The green is guarded by very deep bunkers that stretch from the middle to the left side of the green. Another way to play the hole is to hit the approach shot to the right side of the hole which is accessible to either chip or putt for birdie.

HOLE 10 ROYAL LYTHAM AND ST. ANNES

After completing the par 3 ninth hole which takes you into the village, you are ready to start the back nine of Royal Lytham. The fairway has to be negotiated by driving through the narrow gap between the mounds. If you are able to accomplish this, the fairway opens up a bit for a shot of 140 yards or less. The hole is visually simple and encouraging, preparing you for the difficulty that is to come in the subsequent holes of this wonderful course.

I have found that 10th holes on many courses tend to be afterthoughts and sometimes are close to or almost mirror image a hole on the front nine. It's as if the designer decided to have lunch at the turn and stifled the creative juices for the back nine.

There are some other 10th holes that are also great to play, such as the 10th at Stanford University. The 10th is a straightforward 360-yard par 4 with two bunkers guarding the landing area of the tee shot. It's a hole that Tiger Woods routinely drove when he was playing there.

HOLE 11 SPANISH BAY GOLF LINKS

I am partial to liking this hole because I have made eagle 2 twice on the hole. The hole is a short par 4 of 345 yards with a slight dogleg to the right. The approach is either a 3 wood to the middle of the fairway, or a well-struck driver with a significant cut on the ball. There is a bunker in the fairway that will grab a tee shot of 235-250 yards. The approach shot is a short iron to the green, but the green has a significant slope that must be carried or else the ball will roll off the green. The pin is usually placed in the back position required that the slope must be carried which can require an extra club depending on the condition of the wind.

HOLE 12 PORT MARNOCK GOLF CLUB

Portmarnock's 12th is a wonderful par 3 of 177 yards with the Atlantic Ocean on the right. The hole is defined by the speed of the wind on any particular day, and it is usually blowing hard toward the ocean. It seems that everything, including ball flight, moves toward the ocean, so the tee shot has to be hit well. The hole is a typical links hole, well-bunkered on the left and the right with a large putting surface. It's a challenge to make par here, but very possible.

HOLE 14-DUNES COURSE-MONTERREY PENINSULA GOLF CLUB, PEBBLE BEACH, CALIFORNIA

I am a sucker for links golf and the 14th hole on the Dunes is a spectacular par 3. The back tee box (which is the only way to play it) is 182 yards from the green. The Pacific Ocean is on the right and the wind is always blowing hard from the ocean to the green. Your tee shot has to cover 175 yards to traverse the Pacific, and there is nothing but ocean between you and the green. The real neat part is the Bird Rock turnout is right behind the tee. The 17-mile drive that runs through the Del Monte Forest at Pebble Beach cuts across the ocean from Spanish to Cypress Point before turning inland to the Pebble Beach lodge. Bird Rock is a turnout off the

17-mile drive and a habitat for sea birds and seals. Bird Rock attracts numbers of tourists who stop and take in the fabulous sights of these animals in their own habitat. It also provides an additional attraction of watching golfers tee off from a spot on the rock some 180 yards of carry over the Pacific Ocean. You have your own gallery as you tee off on the 14th hole, so you want to hit a good shot. You have to take the ball over the ocean to keep the ball on the green. You have to actually aim to the drive the ball into the Pacific Ocean, as the prevailing wind will always blow the ball back onto the group. The mental problem is actually taking aim over the Pacific, because if you aim your tee sheet to the ground, the wind will blow the shot at least 10-15 yards to the left of the green. Then you will have to chip the ball back into the wind. This hole would be innocuous in any other spot, as the wind is the biggest factor to place the ball on the green. This hole is the highlight of the round at the Dunes Course.

HOLE 15- CYPRESS POINT CLUB, PEBBLE BEACH, CALIFORNIA

The 15th at Cypress is a beautiful par 3 of usually only 135 yards, with the prevailing wind blowing in from the Pacific Ocean, which is directly to the right of the tee box. The hole is well- bunkered and the scenery is breathtaking, as the Pacific Ocean is the right side of the hole. A well- struck eight iron should result in a green in regulation and no worse than par. It's a nice warm-up for what is to follow on the treacherous 16th at Cypress.

HOLE 16 MONTERREY PENINSULA COUNTRY CLUB-SHORE COURSE

Hole 16 is the first hole on the way in to the clubhouse and is really a birdie hole. The hole is a par 5 that plays between 450-500 yards depending on the tee boxes. The tee shot must carry the waste area between the tee and the fairway of about 180 yards. The hole is dotted with beautiful scenery, bunkers that are there for the long hitters and bunkers guarding the green from center to left of the green. It's possible to get home in two shots and have an eagle putt here, but birdie is really a possibility.

HOLE 17 PEBBLE BEACH GOLF LINKS, PEBBLE BEACH, CALIFORNIA

The hole is one of the most famous holes in links golf and site of Tom Watson's US Open victory over Jack Nicklaus in 1982. Watson holed a bunker shot to birdie the hole and go on to defeat Nicklaus by a shot. Unfortunately, the USGA has "tricked up" this hole for recent US Opens, pushing the tees back to 182 yards where it is very difficult for the professional to hold a shot on the green or go at the pin. At certain times, the hole played over 200 yards into the prevailing wind. The hole is usually played at 160-165 yards, but the green is very long but not very wide and so many well-struck shots will find the bunkers that surround the green.

HOLE 18: OLD COURSE AT ST. ANDREWS

The finishing hole at the Old Course of St. Andrews is wonderful experience as you drive the golf ball into the town. The hole has the widest fairway of any golf course in the world. It is virtually impossible to hit the ball out of bounds, but I'm sure it has been done. The hole measures 345 yards and if the wind is blowing with the ball, it is possible to drive the green or hit it into the "Valley of Sin." When the wind is dead against, it's actually hard to carry the ball over the road, which is about 190 yards off the tee. There has been a lot of drama over the years on this hole, and John Daly won his first British Open here in a playoff over Constantino Rocca. In benign conditions, the green can be driven, but any miss will cause the ball to end up in the infamous Valley of Sin in the front of the green. The Valley of Sin creates a difficult chip shot to get close to the pin. Putting out of the Valley of Sin is not easy and I'm sure three putts is the normal score out of that particular surface.

FAVORITE GOLF COURSE

Many people understand my passion for golf as I describe some of my experiences and vignettes at social occasions. I'm usually stumped and hard-pressed to answer the question about my favorite golf course, since I've played so many wonderful venues. I've also noticed that many other avid golfers have difficulty answering this question. This chapter is an attempt to answer that question.

Before I list the courses, I offer the following criteria as to how I would select my favorite venues:

1. The course offers a good experience to players of all skill levels.
2. The course has an "even" feel to it that it is fair, yet challenging to all players' capability.
3. The course does not have "blind shots or holes." The game is hard enough--you want to be able to see what you're doing and where you're going.
4. The clubhouse and clubhouse facilities are top-notch and steeped in tradition and are noted for service quality.

With those criteria, my favorite golf courses are:

ROYAL LYTHAM AND ST. ANNE'S ENGLAND

The course is a challenging British Open venue with great traditions, and a wonderful place to play. Each hole offers a unique challenge and the front side straddles a rail line. The 9th hole winds into the village, where you could actually drop off your dry cleaning. The front nine is very playable with sort of an even temper.

After the 10th, you had better concentrate, as the wind will come up and you get a mixture of a bit of grinding and relief. The 17th hole is very difficult, as Adam Scott can attest—this is where he surrendered his opportunity to win a British Open --and the 18th is a beautiful hole, well bunkered, and another site where British Open champions have been crowned. David Duval has won here, as well as Tom Lehman.

One of the wonderful things about being at Royal Lytham is that you can stay at the Dormy House on the grounds. The Dormy House is aptly named as a dormitory for staying a night or two in a very functional bedroom without a private bath, giving you the experience of your college days in the dormitory. Dormy House is cozy and comfortable and will prepare you for a fine day on the course. The course's first hole is a par 3 which is highly unusual for any golf course, and it is here where Ian Woosnam was penalized for having an extra driver in his bag for the Final Round of the British Open.

SHORE COURSE-MONTERREY PENINSULA GOLF COURSE

I have a bias toward the Shore Course since I really enjoy seaside golf and you get a number of great holes and ocean view scenery on a number of holes on this course. What I really like about the course is the variety of shots you have to play, with very different looks on many of the holes. The short par 4-5th hole measures a mere 300 yards, but it has bunkering and hazards on the right side of the hole virtually from tee to green. The par 5, 6th hole is a long par 5 winding around to an uphill green. The par 3 7th hole seems virtually impossible, with a carry of at least 200 yards required to hit the green against the prevailing wind. Any shot hit below the hole will run down almost 35 yards from the green.

The course is easy to walk and offers spectacular views of the Pacific Ocean on thirteen of its holes. The course is a pleasure to play and the wind always makes it challenging but fair.

MANNINGS HEATH GOLF CLUB-WEST SUSSEX, ENGLAND

Mannings Heath is a private/public venue in the village of Mannings Heath located in West Sussex, England about 75 miles southeast of London and about 25 miles from Brighton. I was a member there during my tenure as a general manager in England and have fond memories of the place. I believe I was the only American member, and Ian and I played the course every Sunday. Ian was twelve years old and the drive from our home at Walton-On-Thames, Surrey was about forty-five minutes to the club. It was only ten minutes from my office in nearby Horsham. I remember fondly having to stop on the way and feed him before we played, since his appetite was ravenous, and he would down a variety of tra-ditional British fare with a candy bar on the way to the course. We usually played in gray, cloudy weather or even rain, but we always played. I looked forward to spending the time with him after a long week of work and it was also a pleasure to play with him because he was such a good player. When you play against your son, you always win. If you win, you get the satisfaction of beating a good player and if you lose, you feel good about how good your son feels about beating up on his father. It was a great time for both of us. The course was very nice and very well- laid, with generous fairways that reflected the bounce of the heath turf. The course was usually in very good condition unless pummeled by rain. The par 3-7th hole of 190 yards was named the "Punchbowl," as you teed off downhill onto a green completely surrounded by very high mounds. If you missed the green, you would be hitting a very delicate pitch shot down into the punchbowl. The course has very good length and the 18th hole is a treacherous par 4--all uphill to a tiny green that will punish you if it is missed.

TOURNAMENT PLAYERS CLUB, SCOTTSDALE, ARIZONA

TPC Scottsdale is the home of the infamous PGA Tour stop in Scottsdale known for its huge, raucous crowds and very bad fan behavior. The par 3 16th hole is shaped like the Roman Coliseum (for the tournament) as the combatants take aim at the 145-yard hole. Miss the green and the crowd will boo lustily and make fun of the tour player. You'll never see anything like it anywhere else on Tour. This could never happen at a place like Augusta National.

The course is really fun to play because you can use all the clubs in your bag and almost every hole presents a different look. The back nine is very interesting, particularly as you get to the short par 4 17th hole where many amateurs can drive to drive the green. I've been 20-30 yards from the green sometimes. The risk reward of these finishing holes make for an enriching experience and you get a feel for what the professional is thinking when they play the course.

PEBBLE BEACH GOLF CLUB-PEBBLE BEACH CALIFORNIA

I've described a number of the holes on Pebble Beach throughout this book. I am very prejudiced about this course since my second home is two miles from the first tee. I'm also pretty excited about it when I broke par on a very magical day in December with no wind, and when things broke just right for me with three birdies on the front side. The tradition of numerous US Opens and the annual AT&T (formerly Crosby Clambake) is steeped in wonderful traditions. The course is wonderful as you have to take advantage of the first 7 holes if you're going to score well. Then you must survive holes 8-10, where par for the amateur on any of these holes is out-standing. You get a short breadth on number 11 and then grind through 14, finishing the course with marvelous layouts on 15-18. I've played the course so many times that my opinion never changes, and I never tire of playing it. It will host more US Opens and the traditions will be continued.

CYPRESS POINT CLUB-PEBBLE BEACH, CALIFORNIA

Cypress Point is a very special place. The club is in the top three of the most exclusive golf clubs on the face of the earth. I would rank Augusta National and Pine Valley as the other two. As with Augusta National, membership is by invitation only and it's no won-der that many of Cypress' members are also members of Augusta National. There is very little play on the course due to the busy lives of its members who are located all over the globe as CEOs, politi-cians, and power brokers in many different areas. There is no guest play without playing with a member, except on Friday when 5-6 tee times are awarded to guests of members who show up at 8:00 a.m. and tee off by 9:00 a.m. There are no other times for guests to play without members. The course is wonderful to play and it has two breathtaking par 3's back to back--Hole 15 and Hole 16.

The club used to be on the AT&T Pro-AM circuit, but the PGA began to question the membership policies of the club with respect to gender and minorities, and the Cypress board would have none of this. The board felt that the PGA was attempting to inter-fere in the private affairs of a very private club, so The PGA was forced to go elsewhere. We suffered with this decision as Cypress was replaced by the hideous Poppy Hills public golf course run by the NCGA. Many of the professionals labeled Poppy Hills as a "trash pit" and a few years ago, the tournament venue was moved to Monterrey Peninsula Golf Club from Poppy, to the delight of most of the PGA tour players. Apparently somebody got the message, as Poppy Hills has been redone and redesigned, and it reopened about a year ago.

Olympic Club-Lake Course, San Francisco

The Lake Course at Olympic is a marvelous golf course. It has been the home of numerous exciting US Opens and it's a golf course that plays far longer than its measured yardage. I believe this is due its proximity to Lake Merced, the impact of San Francisco's micro climate of early- morning wind and fog, and the resulting impact it has on the fairways. The course can be turned into a ferocious monster just by narrowing the fairway cuts and growing the rough. The USGA does this for the US Open Championship, making par the standard over the four- day event. Amateurs such as myself couldn't break 90 in this condition, and fortunately the fairways are usually kept wide enough to enjoy the course if you can keep it in the fairways. The course offers a mixture of easy holes (No. 1) but mostly the course is pretty difficult due to its length and how it plays. I like the variety of the holes, from the par 4 340-yard finishing hole with a tiny green to the ferocious par 5 17th where the fairway significantly slopes to the right even if the ball is hit right down the middle. The 18th green had to be redone after it played so fast in the 1988 US Open that Tour Player Kirk Triplett threw his ball into the gallery on the hole after watching his putt slide off the green, thereby disqualifying himself after the third round. What I really like about Olympic is that every hole is a strong hole without being unfair or very difficult and you're able to hit almost every club in your bag. The greens are difficult to putt unless you play there often, which most of us can't do. The biggest downside to a membership at Olympic is course availability, since there are a large number of members, which makes weekend tee times difficult to obtain without a lot of preplanning.

Cape Kidnappers, Napier, New Zealand

Cape Kidnappers is a course designed by Tom Doak at the resort called The Farm, about 30 miles north of Napier, New Zealand. Doak is also the designer of Bandon Dunes, Oregon and you get a similar look and feel at Kidnappers. The course is beautifully laid out and can be played by all skill levels with five sets of tee boxes. Fairways are generous, but drives must be placed in the proper position. The 594-yard, par 5 15th hole is the signature hole. The fairway is wide and generous, but falls off a bit on the left side into some menacing rough and heather. The best tee shot is center or slightly right. The interesting shot is the 3rd shot to the green, where the green sits atop a bluff overlooking the ocean. The drop from the green to the ocean is over 400 feet. My approach shot came to rest about 2 yards from rolling down into the caverns below. The view from the green is absolutely spectacular.

Least Favorite or Despised Golf Courses

1. Poppy Hills-Pebble Beach California
2. Old Ranch Golf Club-Long Beach, California
3. Royal Troon-Troon, Scotland
4. Royal Liverpool-Scotland

It is hard to dislike a golf course, but there a few that I don't go out of my way to play. My criteria for disliking a golf course are the following:

1. The course has a number of blind shots. Golf is hard enough and not being able to see where I'm going doesn't leave me with a good feeling.
2. The pro shop staff and general demeanor of the club is arrogant and/or unfriendly. Once again, golf is hard enough,

so you shouldn't have to put up with people who think they are doing you a favor letting you play their golf course.

3. The course is one that I usually never play well. Golf is hard enough, so you shouldn't have to play a course that continuously frustrates you.

POPPY HILLS-PEBBLE BEACH, CALIFORNIA

Poppy Hills is owned by the Northern California Golf Association. This course is less than one mile from my home in Pebble Beach, but I believe it is poorly designed. I haven't played it over ten years and would never play it. It is a public facility run by the Northern California Golf Association so it is heretical to criticize it. It used to be one of the courses used for the Pebble Beach Pro-Am after Cypress Point told the PGA to "take a hike" years earlier. The PGA was critical of Cypress' membership policy, so the club responded by eliminating the course from the Pro-Am venue. The decision by the club was justifiable, but it was unfortunate for the fans and the players to miss out on a fabulous venue. Poppy Hills was selected as the replacement course and the pros hated the course and I heard one of them label it as a "trash pit." It was poorly managed, when I was playing it, and rounds typically took six hours or more. The course is dull, unimaginative, and you can actually hit a ball out of bounds on a few of the holes after it has landed on the green (particularly the par 5 12th). I guess some people actually agree with me, as Poppy Hills is no longer part of the rotation of courses for the AT&T Pro-Am. In fact, I guess even more people agreed with me, as the course was closed for renovation from 2012 to 2014. The course reopened in the summer of 2014, but I have yet to try it. Reviews of the new Poppy Hills remain mixed, so I'm going to leave it on the despised list for now.

Old Ranch Country Club-Long Beach, California

Old Ranch doesn't really meet the criteria for "least favorite" or "despised." I simply can't play well there--ever! There is absolutely nothing wrong with this golf club, as it is an interesting layout with a number of very good holes, particularly on the back nine. I absolutely can't play here and it must be embedded in my mind, since not only can I not break 80--I'm usually lucky to break 90. The course has a number of very interesting holes and the finishing holes are particularly strong. I simply have a mental block playing here, although I am determined to keep trying as the members that bring me there are two of my best friends in the world. I am embarrassed about how poorly I play there and I have no excuse for it. Until I defeat this course, it will continue to be on my "list," but this is my own issue and has nothing to do with the quality of the golf club, its staff, members, or ownership.

Royal Troon and Royal Liverpool

These courses are British Open venues and famous tracks. After enjoying Royal Troon when I first played it in 1992, it makes my list for the arrogance and worst features as I describe on the chapter of British private golf clubs. These courses make you feel you don't belong here, and the staff makes it very obvious. For me, things went downhill quickly when Colin Montgomery's dad, who had been the secretary at Troon, retired. Colin's father was a gracious host, but now the management regard Americans as just an opportunity to charge outrageous amounts of money to play, eat, and buy things there.

Chapter 8
INTERNATIONAL
EXPERIENCES

THE ROYAL CINQUEPORT EXPERIENCE

My close friend Brian Shirley and I have been playing golf together for the last thirty years together since we met at Fairchild
Camera and Instrument Corporation, where Brian worked for me.

I would visit Brian periodically after the family had moved home
from England and we arranged a weekend of the eastern shore of
England where the prize was the opportunity to play at Royal St.
George's. The three-day golf holiday consisted of Saturday at Royal
Cinqueport, Sunday at the Prince's Course and Monday at Royal St.
George's. We were really psyched as we motored up the M-25 and
arrived at the hotel. We looked forward to playing our first round
at Royal Cinqueport. We didn't realize what was about to happen.

We walked into the pro shop and proceeded to give our names
and our tee time and Brian offered his credit card to secure payment
and get the process started. And then it began: "We don't accept credit cards, sir--only cash," stated the man behind the counter. It was a
stern, unfriendly, almost grotesque statement. It was a statement that

was intended to engender fear and total lack of any regard for a customer. After all, Royal Cinqueport was a private club and what are the likes of you two doing here anyway? Brian stated that he knew of no such requirement when he booked the tee time and did not have sufficient cash on his person to pay the greens fees. Again the attendant looked down on him as if to say "not my problem." Brian offered his business card and he would certainly pay by check, as was customary at many establishments and clubs in England. The response was a terse "absolutely not, cash only." Brian then proceeded to tell him that he had brought his friend all the way from California to play here and could they please accommodate him or else would they turn us away from playing at all after we had just driven some 200 miles from London to get here for this round. Again a look of disdain and disgust, "I cannot help you, sir--cash only." Brian was hurt and embarrassed and I was simply flabbergasted and couldn't believe what was happened. Brian and I had played at some very snotty places such as Royal Liverpool and others I won't mention here, but this was the ultimate put-down. Brian turned to me and said "There's no choice; I'll have to drive into town and get to a bank and secure the cash." I was really embarrassed for him, but I readily agreed.

It doesn't end here--Brian came back with the cash and paid the greens fees. Our tee time was past, but we were "allowed" to go… and then came the final straw (or a prelude to the final straw). We walked to the first tee to the back tees of the course (championship tees) to play its full yardage and you'd think the two of us had just murdered someone. As we walked to the back tee the entire pro shop emptied with the shop attendant and his boss and the professional and lord knows who else to tell us that there was no way that we would be able to play from the back tees. Those tees were very special and used only for competitive play and therefore "you" lowly hacks could not play from them. I couldn't believe it…the ultimate in arrogance.

The last straw—after our round on a very ordinary links course—we were not allowed to enter the clubhouse. I believe the place was frequented by Peter Allis, the famous British golfer and BBC/ABC golf commentator, and I've also wondered what he would have thought or said of our experience.

Royal Cinqueport—overrated, arrogant, and discourteous.

PLAYING IN JAPAN

It's pretty well known that the Japanese love the game of golf and are genuinely addicted to the game. Golf in Japan is a very expensive proposition, even in today's depressed economic times. Japan's economy was riding a wave of spectacular success fueled by its capability in technology, and golf became the entertainment vehicle and popular pastime. Golf club membership fees soared into the millions for a membership and greens fees were beyond the reach of the average salaryman. It's pretty common knowledge that the Japanese love golf but during this period of Japanese prosperity, golf was "king" in Japan. Country club memberships in private clubs were in the $500 to $700 thousand range and many were over $1 million. This was the "bubble" period in Japan when real estate prices skyrocketed and the country's economy ruled the world. Books were written by Japanese authors and economics that Japan's technology would soon rule the world. Golf during this period was booming.

For me, golf in Japan was a big ordeal. On the weekends we usually played on Saturday and sometimes would play on Saturday and then make the 4:30 flight home to San Francisco, which would arrive at approximately 9:00 a.m. the same day. There were many trips like this where we actually played two rounds of golf—one in Japan and one at home when we landed. I actually did this on December 7, 1991, the 50th anniversary of Pearl Harbor-- I have two stamps in my passport: departing Japan and arriving in the United States.

Golf for me in Japan was a big ordeal. It was normally a full day that began at 6:00 a.m. for a car pickup since the courses were 1-2 hours away. Since there is very little land in Japan, a number of golf courses are located in the same place in rural areas. The courses tended to be very similar: neat, but not with a lot of imagination. In recent times US architects have been commissioned to design some new courses and a little variety has crept in, but I found most of the courses I played on very boring and forgettable. I did have one very nice experience in Hiroshima, which was the last time I played in Japan.

After you arrive at the course, you go through a very formal check-in process. You are greeted by a number of female attendants, who whisk your clubs out of your car, and then you register for the day's activities. There are so many employees taking care of you that it's no wonder things are so expensive. The registration procedure is similar to checking into a hotel, with fees paid (I never had to pay), locker key issued, and off you go to the locker room. Japan is so safe--I don't know why locker keys are even necessary. Of course you proceed to wash up and get ready for some breakfast. The Japanese do not do American breakfast very well. American food is not their style of eating, so the traditional Japanese breakfast of some soup, dried fish etc. is available. Japanese bread is very "sad" and is like a pile of dough with no taste, so I would avoid it at any cost. American breakfasts in Japan are universally bad all over the country, not just at Japanese country clubs. After breakfast you might have the luxury of hitting a few golf balls or warming up. Tee time is 9:30…remember this all started at 6:00 a.m. Finally, you move to the first tee and despite the fact that you're at a private country club, you feel like you're at the local municipal public course in the US. Every eight minutes, a foursome tees off. You wince as you now realize you're heading into the golf Twilight Zone of a 6+ hour round of golf. The female caddy has all four bags, along with towels, tees, markers, and the lot on a cart that could double as a food purveyor on the streets of New York City. She doesn't read greens and can't help you with club selection. Her English is rather limited to the sounds of "Nice shotto" or "Nice putt." It's almost impossible to lose a ball on a Japanese golf course, unless you plunk one in the myriad water hazards that dot most of the courses. After a grueling three hours for the first nine holes, you are required to return to the clubhouse for "lunch." Lunch is not a fifteen-minute break or a hot dog and a Coke at the turn. It is a formal sit-down of a full Japanese lunch. It's impossible to decline and it's impossible to eat light and it will take sixty minutes no matter what. Why? You have a designated tee time that is ninety minutes from when you entered the clubhouse for lunch. At the end of this laborious exercise I find it amazing that many participants actually nap before moving to the 10th tee. Me, I'm chewing my nails and can't wait to go. For me a round of golf with a foursome that exceeds three hours and forty-five minutes is totally exasperating. We approach the 10th tee at 1:00 p.m. Remember this all started at 6:00 a.m. The pace of play is aggravating and slow. Of course I push our group because I play fast naturally, but it really doesn't help…we just wait longer on the next tee. At 4:45 p.m. the last putt is dropped and a round of six hours and forty-five minutes is complete. I am a total basket case, but we're not done. Off to the clubhouse for the invariable 19th hole consisting of beer and fresh peas. After an hour of the settling of all the myriad bets--which requires a supercomputer to figure out—we head for the bath. All I know is that I shot 82 and that a lot of Japanese yen changed hands. The bath was soothing, but now we are finally about to leave with the inverse process of checkout—once again, just like the hotel we turn in our locker key, our clubs summoned, our female caddy places the clubs in the trunk and off we go. I arrive at the hotel at 9:00 p.m.…totally exhausted. That is the norm for golf in Japan.

I did have a memorable experience in 2004 in the town of Hiroshima. I was now the CEO of a public company in the semi-conductor testing business and was meeting the President of my customer Elpida Memory. Elpida is a leading memory chip company, with a large factory in Hiroshima. I had actually never been to Hiroshima in all the times I had visited Japan, so I didn't know what to expect. The hotel was spartan at best and my Japanese manager and I were going to play with the president and his head of the engineering department on Sunday. Unlike the experience I described previously, this was a different experience. We arrived at the Hiroshima Golf Club on a very hot and humid day in August. It was going to be unbearably hot, but I had this experience before and had brought an extra shirt with me. The club was magnificent and the personnel very friendly. I needed golf clubs to play with and when they brought the clubs, I was flabbergasted…these clubs looked like they had been in somebody's closet for the past thirty years. I turned to my manager and said "I can't play with these things--I'll just play out of your bag." A few minutes went by and after I came out from washing up, the head professional came up to me with a bag of clubs that were very nice. In fact, they were Taylor Made irons and the driver was an R-7, which was exactly what I used at home. What I didn't realize at the time was that those clubs were his personal clubs, so I was really taken aback by the gesture. I decided I needed to thank him somehow and then I remembered. In my shoe bag there were two medallions from Pebble Beach Golf Links which double as bag tags. I went back to my locker, took the medallions, and gave them to the professional as a token of my gratitude for letting me use his clubs. I told him, "I don't think you'll find any of these in Japan," and thanked him. He was absolutely over the moon over this gesture and it really fired me up as we went out to play. I had a great round at Hiroshima Country Club, with great company and a golf course that I would count as the best one I ever played in Japan. A thoroughly enjoyable experience…and…it was a 4 ½ hour round without the lengthy lunch break in between. Unfortunately, this experience was the exception and one that I have relished ever since then.

If you travel by train or car throughout Japan, you'll notice a bunch of green netting that dots the skyline in virtually any city or municipality you pass by. The green netting is the surroundings of the Japanese driving range. The driving range is the way most people in Japan play golf, since it is the only readily accessible way to swing a golf club. Some Japanese have never been on a golf course and their only experience is the driving range. The driving range is very different from the American phenomenon. The driving range in Japan is a unique experience. I used to frequent the one in the town of Narita, which is the site of the international airport. We had a facility there employing about 400 people. In the mid-eighties we would conduct the business of the company there. In order to keep the golf game sharp, I would go over to the Narita driving range. The range is impeccably clean and every stall is perfect. All the tees are the same height and the balls are continuously cleaned by an underground cleaning system. As balls are hit, they are collected and run underground, washed, and returned to the ball machines that dispense the balls. There are no rickety trucks or snow plow trucks covered in mesh covering to protect the driver on a Japanese driving range. There is no Tin Cup experience here. Most of the ranges are only 220 yards out, since it's quite intoxicating to hit the balls out of the range and over the netting, since most Japanese amateurs cannot accomplish this. Balls hit as hooks or slices will carom off the netting into the collection areas. Target areas are everywhere with clear yardage markers in meters.

Japan is an extraordinary place and a society of contradictions, especially in the way they treat foreigners. Honesty in Japan is central to the fabric of the society, but there can be excursions, especially when golf is involved. I had an intriguing experience while traveling on business to Japan in 1987. During the 1980s, the Japanese were the kings of the semiconductor experience and our company supplied equipment to that industry. We spent a lot of time in Japan during this period and I traveled to Japan an average of ten times a year during the 1980s. On one of those trips we decided to bring our golf clubs to Japan—we were going to play on Saturday in Japan after concluding our business, but we really took our clubs because we planned on flying home through Hawaii and playing a few rounds on Oahu at the Hilton resort Arnold Palmer course. After the twelve-hour flight from San Francisco, we boarded the "airport limousine" bus for the three-hour bus ride to our hotel in the Shinjuku section of Tokyo where our headquarters were. We were the last stop on this wonderful trip, which was very difficult after the twelve-hour flight. The first stop on the bus was the Shinjuku train station, where most of the passengers disembarked. The remaining three stops were hotels. The Century Hyatt Hotel was the last stop, where we were staying. Our luggage and golf clubs were on the bus but as we got off at the Century Hyatt—the only baggage left on the bus was our luggage—the golf clubs were gone. We were pretty upset and asked the driver what happened to our golf clubs—of course, he mistakenly took them off the bus at the Shinjuku train station. Before we could even express our frustration at this situation, the driver shrieked and said to us, "Please wait here, I'll be right back." The Shinjuku train station was at least ten minutes away, so the likelihood of our clubs being located seemed slim and none. The sincerity of the driver touched me and I decided to give him the benefit of the doubt. We didn't have many other choices. Incredibly, he returned in about twenty minutes with a big smile on his face and golf clubs on the bus. This could happen only in Japan…anywhere else, the clubs would have been taken.

Of course, the Japanese bubble economy burst in the mid-'90s and some golf courses went out of business. Initiation fees at private country clubs cratered to historic lows from the $500,000-$700,000 and up to less than $100,000. Japan's semiconductor business went into the tank as they underinvested and lost out to the upstarts in Korea and Taiwan and some resurgence from US companies. Golf is as popular as ever, but just like the rest of Japan—things are flat or declining.

2010 TRIP TO ENGLAND

It was 2010 and I decided to visit Brian in the second week of April, just after Ian and I had completed seeing the Final Four in Indianapolis, Indiana. It was great to see Brian and Jacky again, as Brian was now well enough to exercise his magical swing. I have a set of clubs here in England, which are Titleist blade irons which I bought in 1990 and left here in England as my UK set of clubs. Unfortunately, the woods were Calloway vintage and had become virtually extinct in the US, so I needed new woods. Last year when I was here in Somerset, England in February we played only one round, at Brian's local club, Wheat Hill. At the time the grips on those Titleist irons had never been changed and were thoroughly worn--and lack of use and storage in the vineyard garage didn't help matters either. Brian had the irons regripped and the clubs were almost as good as new. A venue was set to play the 2010 Ryder Cup course: Celtic Manor in South Wales, and two private clubs which were both links courses—Burnham and Bellows, and Sauton Golf Club.

After a refreshing four-hour nap after my journey from San

Francisco we set out for South Wales and Celtic Manor. We arrived and checked into the hotel at Celtic Manor. The hotel is relatively new, as is the golf course, but it was part of a longer-term development program. The older hotel, called Manor House, seemed more stately and refined than the newer variety where we stayed. I felt that the standard was slightly below "top notch," but we had a nice dinner at the Manor House restaurant. After getting ripped for a $50 breakfast (each) we set out for our 9:40 tee time at Celtic Manor. The place is pretty big, with two additional golf courses as well, but only Celtic Manor was behind its own gates. The course is definitely well-suited for the Ryder Cup with significant length for the big hitters, and the course will play at about 7500 yards. It was pretty cold when we played, and the wind was up. I liked the course and found it to be quite scenic, with a good variety of shots for the skilled player. We got round the front nine in less than 2 hours, including the 616 par 5 ninth hole. The back nine is a gradual climb and was pretty pleasant through the 14th hole. We found the 15th hole to be an afterthought and aberrant to the quality of the course. The hole is about 380 yards' dogleg to the right, with trees hugging the right side of the fairway, and anything hit to the right will disable any approach to the green. A small pond guards the elevated green about 80 yards and anything hit short of the green will roll into the pond. We didn't like this hole at hole, but understood that it could be potentially very exciting for the professionals, because we thought someone like Phil Mickelson potentially could drive the ball over all the trees on the right and try to drive the green and eliminate the elevation of the hole altogether. After the 15th we kept climbing up since we were carrying our clubs and walking and it became pretty tiresome but we finally made it up to the 18th hole, which we really liked. Of course we liked it because we both smacked 280-yard drives down the middle of the fairway. We were playing the hole from 535-yard tees, while I think the pros will be playing the hole from almost 600 yards. It's a typical Ryder Cup finish with a daunting second shot over the pound to another elevated green. Any shot that's short of the elevated green will end up in the pond. We laid up short of the pond (of course) and hit wedges to the elevated green, two-putted for pars, and celebrated the end of a nice round of golf. Once the spectator stands are installed for the Ryder Cup, the course will have a complete differently look from what we saw, but it is a venue that will be very similar to other Ryder Cup venues--although the Cup course for 2014 at Gleneagles was different from this venue and I believe provided a more interesting test for the professionals.

THE BRITISH PRIVATE GOLF CLUB

Before I go on to describe the two links courses we played during this trip, I have some comments about private British golf clubs. This will not be a flattering description, but visitors from the United States will find things very different in the UK from the United States in a number of ways. There are a few private clubs in the US that have some of these characteristics, but in the UK, these are quite widespread.

1. The visitor is made to feel inherently unwelcome, as if you are entering some hallowed ground (maybe heaven). There is an air of inherent unwelcomeness.
2. The parking lot (or car park) is littered with restricted car parking for visitors, and signs everywhere with reserved parking for the club secretary, men's captain (whatever that is), lady captain, professional, and so on. At Sauton we even saw signs for "committee parking."
3. The locker rooms are generally old and decrepit and despite this state of decrepitude, these people make you think that

you are entering the Taj Mahal. Visitors are clearly viewed with disdain, as they are allowed only to change their shoes in the "Visitors" area. Signs are posted everywhere as to what you can do--or put more correctly "what you can't do" by "Order of the Management" (whoever they are). I don't believe grade school children are subjected to such written instruction.

4. After you have had the parking lot and locker room experience, you are now ready to enter the world of the professional golf shop. This is usually a mixed bag, as some of the clubs are welcoming and helpful. However, I find most of them continue to view you with disdain, and how dare you come visit our hallowed ground for a round of golf. We are happy to rip you for the green fees, but that's not the least of it.

5. You will place some little unbearable ugly tag that proves to the world that you have paid your greens fees so that the "starter" can verify that you haven't emerged from the woods to play. God forbid you have forgotten anything or need any ancillary equipment. You will actually PAY for golf tees, pencils (20 pence each), yardage book (5 pounds), even a broken-down hand cart to roll your clubs around during the round (2 pounds).

6. So now you have paid and you want to warm up a bit. Oh well, dig back into your pocket for more money for driving range balls. Until recently (in my experience) there were no driving ranges in private clubs—you would take your own shag bag, hit the balls, and pick them up yourself—just what you want to do when you're on vacation.

7. Now you've been welcomed, you've paid (for everything) and now you would like to hit some putts to get the feel of the

greens before you start your round. One of the first things you notice at some clubs is that there are more signs of what you can and cannot do, "no chipping," "no standing," and one of the real gems--"quiet please."

By this time, you wonder why you came here in the first place, but you're used to being treated with disdain and total lack of courtesy here and you are finally ready to take the first tee. One more obstacle—the starter—who looks down at you, measures you up and once again with consistent treatment, looks at you as if you were from another planet. Another final chapter of pablum about the "do's" and "don'ts" are elucidated as if you were indeed a child who had never lifted a golf club in your life. Off you go and you hit the first tee ball and forget about the last hour of pain and suffering.

If you want the exact opposite experience of all of this…play in Ireland, where they really know how to treat people.

Unfortunately the English private club golf scourge is trademarked throughout the Empire where the English exported the game. Today you can find the same ridiculous signs and traits in Spain, Portugal, Singapore, Hong Kong, and Japan. I haven't made it to South Africa, so I can't comment, but it's probably true there to.

THE 2009 BRITISH OPEN AT TURNBERRY

The 2009 Open Championship at Turnberry, in my opinion, is one of the greatest moments in the history of golf and all of sport. This opinion would be disputed and disregarded by the pundits of sport, but I believe it differentiates golf as a sport from any other endeavor.

The event will be known for the person who actually came in second, Tom Watson, rather than the winner, Stewart Cink. Watson was seeking to win his 6th Open Championship at the age of sixty, which would have made him the oldest winner of a major championship, an accomplishment that would be viewed as highly implausible in the modern era of sport. I take these moments very seriously, as I find that today's sporting public easily forgets the achievements of athletes in past years once these athletes have retired.

Turnberry was a good venue for Watson to make a run at another Open Championship. He had won there before and the length of the course was still within his competitive capabilities. He had a lot of confidence coming into the tournament and thought he had a realistic chance of making a serious run at victory. All of these situations were true as Tom played very well, holding the lead for most of the event. Day by day, hole by hole, shot by shot, putt by putt--he maintained his confidence and the lead. We're going to fast-forward to the 18th hole, the 72nd hole of the tournament, with Watson holding a one-shot lead. Stewart Cink, alone in second place, had a terrific day, along with a few fortuitous bounces, and waited alongside the 18th hole for Watson's arrival. Watson needed a par to win to achieve this modern miracle. It seemed that anyone who watching or even thinking about the Open Championship was pining for Watson to pull it off, including me and millions of TV viewers all over the world. The collective "karma" of the golfing universe was begging for this feat to be accomplished. Watson deserved it" he had played well and was in a terrific position to make it happen. His drive on the 18th hole was well-placed, finding the fairway, so the first big step was accomplished. All he needed to do now was to put the ball on the green, two putt, and walk off with his sixth Open Championship at age sixty. He selected an 8 iron from 181 yards as the hole was a bit downwind and the green was rock-hard from the wind and sunshine. The shot was off, flying straight and true, and then took a terrible bounce as it approached the green. The club was struck impeccably and should have resulted in a good position on the green. The ball took a horrible bounce and began to run hard and fast over the green as if an evil god were sweeping it with a broom--and there it went, past the hole and over the green. The crowd gasped and announcers had their mouths open. Everything just stopped--how could a shot like that end up in this place? The ball was about 18 feet past the pin, a depression which would require the most delicate of pitch shots to get close. Most professionals can get this shot up and down eight times out of ten, but not when the shot is to achieve something that has never been done in golf--win the Open Championship at age sixty. The entire golfing world was descending on this pitch shot. When things like this happen, good shots become bad ones, the world starts to move very fast and you lose self control-whether it's for the $5 Nassau or the Open Championship—you're unhappy that the gods of golf have put you in this position and you now have to make the shot of your life. The odds are stacked against you, the crowd, the pressure, the stakes—it's just too much. It happened to Bernard Langer at the Ryder Cup and too many others many times before. Watson just couldn't concentrate fully on the shot that he had probably made countless times before. If it was a different tournament such as a Senior PGA event or a practice round, I'm sure he would have knocked it a few inches from the hole. After all, that is what professionals do. He seemed tentative over the chip shot, still hot and angry inside, trying to control his emotions as he tried to convert the shot. The shot clipped off the wedge and he knew it was over--the ball nestled past the hole between 4-5 feet with a devilish break that should never have come into play. He was clearly disappointed and disgusted…and now the internal body clock speds up again. Now he had to make this putt to win the Open Championship. He was angry. It was unfair--he hit the best 8 iron of the day, bounced it in front of the green (as planned), and it ended up in a horrible place over the green. He shouldn't be in this position, but the rest of him was trying to calm the nerves and concentrate at the task at hand. It couldn't happen—in situations like this, the mind begins to conjure up images of many missed 4-footers in the past where other events were lost or caused him to lose his position. The other part of the mind tries to remember all of the 4-footers that were made to win tournaments, but the negative vibes from the mind continue to dominate. The amazing thing in this situation is that Watson was one of the best players in the world, who had been through this situation many times before beating the likes of Jack Nicklaus and having the exhilaration that none of us could ever experience in golf. He had been to the top of the mountain and held the prize--what was another 4-footer? The enormity of the prize was just too much to fathom…there was just too much positive energy from the golfing public that wanted to wish this putt into the hole. I sat there watching it on TV and could hardly look. I knew he was going to miss it--I had seen him miss too many of those, and magnified by these circumstances, it was simply too much to ask of anybody. As the putter blade went back, I could just picture the anguish that was about to appear and the disappointment to follow as the putt rolled away not even close to the hole. The crowd let out a collective groan in extreme disappointment. The TV audience led out a collective groan--it just wasn't right and fair--it was supposed to end in a fairy tale like fashion, like a Michael Jordan jump shot at the buzzer to win an NBA championship. The gods of golf be cursed for letting the iron shot run through the green. The ensuing playoff was really unnecessary; Watson was so unnerved and upset that the playoff was played at warp speed. I'm sure he remembers very little about the playoff as Cink crushed him as the match play between the two of them was not even competitive. Despite the outcome, Watson will be more famous for not winning the 2009 Open Championship than Stewart Cink will be for winning it. I'm sure that very few people in five years' time will remember that Stewart Cink won that Open Championship at Turnberry.

BALLYBUNION-1982

My first experience at golf in Ireland was with Ian, Brian, and his brother Roy. Ian was eleven years old and about 4' 6" but he could hold his own on a championship golf course, with a handicap of 9. The country was beautiful and green but it was pouring rain as we disembarked the aircraft. It was during the days of the Gulf War and tensions in Northern Ireland were still high, so we were a bit bemused as our Aer Lingus flight from Heathrow was escorted into the gate with an armed personnel carrier.

Brian had rented a car and off we set on a long journey round the Irish coast to arrive at Ballybunion. The next day we would set out and play 36 holes over Ballybunion's two courses. Accommodation and hospitality at Ballybunion was outstanding and since this was my first trip to Ireland, I would find that it was a typical experience, as the Irish really know to treat a guest. Tom Watson is revered at Ballybunion and he is the honorary Professional of the Golf Club. We were all pretty excited about the next day, but our hopes would soon be dashed. Our first tee time at the Old Course was early, about 7:30 a.m., and it was absolutely pouring down rain. Worse yet—visibility was nearly zero. On the first tee we could barely make out the cemetery that adjoins the first fairway. It was raining so hard and horizontal that we had to keep our heads down just to move. The weather ruined the round...we couldn't concentrate on a course that isn't easy to begin with, and none of us had the experience of the mounding that shapes the course. The first 18 was a test of survival and we survived it, but I have no memory of the course, since there was no visibility. We simply tried to execute shots that would stay in the fairway. Our spirits remained high as we trudged off for lunch. It had poured (teemed) virtually the entire 18 holes. Not all was lost and we wondered what would happen in the afternoon playing New Ballybunion. Magically the skies cleared and the sun began to shine, and we were really psyched to play the afternoon round. Ian, at age eleven, was a real trooper and determined as well. We decided to play a match and Ian and Brian would play against Roy and me. It was 1991 and Brian was the best player, with a handicap of 8. We decided to play a one-best ball match with Brian giving us 1 per side. We were very disappointed with the condition of New Ballybunion, as it was nothing like Old in terms of neatness and the roll of the greens. The course had only been open a few years and was definitely not the test of Old--but then again, we really didn't see Old. The match was tight and we got to the 14th hole all even. Brian had the honor and decided to tee the ball off from in front of the tee markers. He claimed that the teeing ground was unplay-able—it was pretty ratty--and proceeded to hit his drive down the middle of the fairway. Roy and I said nothing and as soon as he hit the ball announced, "Loss of hole--hitting the ball from a place that is not the teeing ground." Brian looked up and became pretty upset, citing that the ground was unplayable and that if Roy didn't agree he should have said something. The debate became heated and I said I would take responsibility to obtain the right ruling, which I never did. We proceeded to win the hole anyway but Brian was clearly upset. The match ended in "all square" and we decided to settle it on the practice putting green, which Roy and I won, but the argument has gone on for years.

PUBLIC GOLF IN THE UK

Weekends at first were tough, since Ian and I were used to play-ing golf together at a private country club. We had no entry into private clubs-- although that would come later--so we started hit-ting the public driving ranges and the public golf courses. A place called Silvermere was close to our area. The weather was usually gray, damp, and cold, but we had to keep our games intact so we would go out on Saturday and Sunday for a few hours of batting balls around. It was pretty bad, but we persevered and actually played Silvermere about twice a month. The public golf courses were similar in the UK to the US version, and the UK probably taught the US the ghastly techniques of public golf courses. The course entry was covered in a myriad of signs telling you what you could or could not do every step of the way as if you were a child taking your first step or uttering your first word. Rules and signage were everywhere. Some tees on the course had synthetic mats—another wonderful feature exported to the eastern part of the US. We didn't have this in California, but we do have the signs, the rules, and of course the horrible slow play caused by ignorant players and sending foursomes off every eight minutes instead of twelve minutes.

RICHMOND GOLF CLUB

Brian and I spent many wonderful days playing this old club in Ealing, which is the Southwestern part of London. Brian and his brother Roy were members of the club and we started playing together almost as soon as I became a resident in Surrey. It was only about a half-hour drive on a weekend morning when we would play pretty early. Brian was usually late and the state of my game at that time required some warm-up. Unfortunately, when I started playing there in 1991 there was only a cage where you could swing and hit a few balls into a mat. Not exactly warming up, I would say. The course was short, but really fun to play, especially when it was quiet, as the only noise you would hear is the consistent droning of 747s as the course was on a flight path into Heathrow Airport.

Richmond is quite a nice part of London and the club had no markings, as its entrance was down at the end of a private lane. You drove in and crossed the first and the eighteenth hole, so you had to be careful that no one was on the tee, or your car would become target practice. My game was okay during this period but I was playing off a "shaky" 10 handicap. It was rather unlike most British private clubs as its clubhouse was a national monument and therefore devoid of the ridiculous signage that dots most English private clubs telling you what you can do and what you can't do at every turn. Richmond was stately, old but elegant, and the golf course was quite tidy. I believe Nick Price, PGA Champion, might have held the course record with 60 and certainly this was possible for the professional, as the course ran only about 6100 yards. Like most of British golf, the course's difficulty would be determined by the weather, with the frequent wind, rain, and cold that plague the golfer in the UK. You have to be willing to play in these conditions, or you won't get to play much. The course was very enjoyable to play and while no hole actually stands out as terribly difficult or terribly easy, you would have to say that the course was a true test of golf. You could score well on it, but you could also be significantly penalized for errant shots, as the course is a parklands layout with significant woods and trees. Members were very interesting people, as many of them were in the theater or the movies, as the Pinewood Studios were nearby. I believe the membership was a terrific distribution of all walks of the London gentry with businessmen, doctors, and lawyers mixed in with theatrical types. They all seemed to have a profound dislike of the American, but they seemed to tolerate me and always treated me well. The club was made famous or infamous by a piece in *Sports Illustrated* years ago, as it did not cease operations during the World War II despite the pounding taken in the city of London and surrounding areas. The following temporary local rules are printed here:

Richmond Golf Club: Temporary Rules 1941

1. Players are asked to collect bomb and shrapnel splinters to save these causing damage to the mowing machines.

2. In competitions, during gunfire or while bombs are falling, players may take shelter without penalty for ceasing play.

3. The position of known delayed action bombs are marked by red flags at a reasonable, but not guaranteed, safe distance therefrom.

4. Shrapnel and/or bomb splinters on the fairways or in bunkers, within a club's length of a ball, may be moved without penalty, and no penalty shall be incurred if a ball is thereby caused to move accidentally.

5. A ball moved by enemy action may be replaced or, if lost or destroyed, a ball may be dropped not nearer the hole without penalty.

6. A ball lying in a crater may be lifted and dropped not nearer the hole, preserving the line to the hole, without penalty.

7. A player whose stroke is affected by the simultaneous explosion of a bomb may play another ball. Penalty: one stroke.

I don't think you will find this type of situation in the annals of the USGA, but people at Richmond take their golf seriously.

The club is as vibrant today, although it's been five years since I've been there, as it was in 1941. Brian since moved away and finally had to give up his membership since the club would not grant him non-resident status. (an entirely different matter, which is almost as complex as the Temporary Rules of 1941).

Italy

I don't know too many people who have played in Italy, but I have really enjoyed the experience. The name "Bronson" is English and my father married into a huge Italian family, "Iovino." I was raised Italian and we lived in New Haven, Connecticut in the Italian Wooster Square neighborhood. I went to the local Catholic grammar school and I was the only student in the entire school whose name ended in a consonant. We lived with my first- generation Italian grandparents and it was a great experience and a very happy childhood for me.

Linda and I have been vacationing in Italy every year for the last six years and have developed a love affair with Florence and the region of Tuscany. Our experiences are not unique, as many of our friends and acquaintances feel the same way. The third time we planned our trip to Tuscany, I decided that I had to play golf in Italy and started researching where to play. I selected Ugolino Golf Club just outside of Florence. We always use Abercrombie & Kent to make all of our arrangements such as hotels, transportation, and museum tickets etc. A&K were taken aback when I requested the golf arrangement at Ugolino, as most vacationers don't go to Tuscany to play golf. My Italian, which was pretty good as a child, was pretty stale, so my language skills were dated and I had to get by as best I could. I never travel with golf clubs for trips like this, so I needed clubs to rent and all of the other logistical arrangements. Golf in Italy is a rich man's sport and very exclusive and aristocratic. My driver pulled into the club along a beautiful tree-lined road into a private enclave. My big surprise came when I signed in to play and asked for my rental clubs. The clubs were horrible at best--old and rusty, but there wasn't much I could do about it, especially with my poor Italian. I was in no position to complain, so I trudged off to play by myself since there was hardly anyone on the course and this was a Saturday! I really liked the course with its pleasant rolling hills, uneven lies, and tree-lined fairways. The course is very narrow, with very little room for error on either side, as the course measures only 6200 yards from the back tees. I had a nice round, despite the clubs, and a great time. I complained to A&K about the arrangements, but they really didn't have the experience to understand what my complaints were about—namely the quality of the golf clubs.

I felt I was the only American that had played the course that year. I complained about the equipment rental with A&K and we went back to Tuscany the following year. This time was totally different. It was as if they recognized me, although I hadn't been there in a year. They welcomed me and instead of dragging out a set of rusty 1950 vintage clubs, out came a brand- new set of Taylor Made irons and metal woods. I was psyched to have a familiar set of tools and proceeded to play very well with two other members. It was a wonderful crisp sunny Saturday and the course was very quiet. When the round was completed, my Italian slipped as I thought I was ordering a simple plate of pasta and ended up with a multiple-course meal, which I couldn't finish.

I would return again the following year with Meredith in tow to be my companion. I needed the company since I was now on vacation in Tuscany with five women—Linda, Cynthia, and Sarah (my sisters-in-law), Meredith, and Leslie Melman (a close friend of the family). I needed a break from all of them and the experience at Ugolino was even more special this time with Meredith being there.

CHINA

It's hard to believe, but playing golf at Mission Hills in Shenzen, China is an amazing experience. There are a total of twelve golf courses there, which means that there are nearly 1,000 people playing golf at one time in this immense facility. Shenzen is a large industrial city about one hour by car from Hong Kong. The golf courses were designed by famous contemporary professionals such as Nick Faldo, Ernie Els, etc. The pro shop is the largest of its kind with an ability to service over 3,000 people. I had the opportunity to play there on a business trip with local executives on one of my trips to China. We were playing on both days of the weekend. The problem for me is that I had significant pain in right elbow and could hardly lift my right arm at all on the previous weekend. I couldn't account for how this had happened, but I couldn't eat without pain and shaving and combing my hair were agonizing. I was leaving for China on the following Wednesday, so I had to do something. I contacted my doctor, who examined me and we decided that I would need a cortisone injection to make the trip. I never had a cortisone injection, but I was desperate and in terrible pain. By Tuesday, I had some flexibility in the joint and left for China on Wednesday. Our first game was Saturday morning and I really shouldn't have played. I had some flexibility, but really couldn't play normally. I told my guests that I really couldn't play, but that I would try. I decided to play from the ladies' tees with a seven iron, pitching wedge and a putter. I played that way the entire day and shot 84 as I hit every 7 iron 150 yards and used the pitching wedge for all the other shots. I found the greens to be very poor and extremely slow and almost decided to putt with the 7 iron.

On Sunday, I felt much better and played from the regular tees but used irons the entire round--except I felt good enough toward the end of the round to hit a few drivers and 3 woods. The Sunday round began at 3:00 p.m., so I asked my guests how could we possibly finish the round—there answer—"Night Golf." I didn't realize that Mission Hills had lights and that you could easily play all evening if you had to. Unless you hit a ball into the trees, there was no visibility problem. I wouldn't rate Mission Hills as a golf destination for me—it's too crowded, there is too much bad golf and it takes too long—five to six hours. I found the courses that I played rather easy and unimaginative, but enjoyable to play.

Chapter 9
GOLF EQUIPMENT

Golf equipment is like audio gadgets and personal technology equipment. It is designed to be the latest state of the art and quickly within a year or two is deemed obsolete and irrelevant. The problem with golf equipment is not with the equipment, but with the users of the equipment. There is no substitute for good swing technique and fundamentals, but golf instruction is very much like the equipment. Golf instruction also becomes obsolete very quickly and we'll cover this in another chapter. Advances in equipment generally benefit only one class of golfer: the professional and low-handicap amateur. If you watch the old black and white films of Jack Nicklaus, Arnold Palmer, and Sam Snead on *Shell's Wonderful World of Golf*, you would discover that they hit persimmon wooden clubs almost 300 yards off the tee. Golf courses were shorter and not as well-kept in those years, so by and large nothing much has changed in scoring. As equipment has changed, so too has the golf ball, and courses have had to be lengthened to challenge the professional.

My biggest weakness in my golf game has always been length off the tee. This is caused by poor fundamentals in the golf swing. What really bugs me is that the rest of the clubs in my bag go as far as most amateurs and my peers, while my driving is consistently

20-30 yards behind my playing partners. The invention and marketing of the first metal wood by Taylor Made was a godsend to my game, as I was able to retire all of my persimmon drivers which I uniformly hit poorly most of the time. The metal wood seemed to be forgiving and the dreaded slice or hook became a thing of the past for me and I was longer than I had ever been. Since the introduction of the metal wood, I have been on the quest for the Holy Grail of Driving Distance and have purchased over thirty drivers over the years. I believe I have purchased every Taylor Made driver ever made including Rocket balls, R-11, R-9, R-7, R-5 and all of their parents. I don't have all of the Titleist drivers, but I have a lot of them, including the new 910-D. I have them with different shafts and loft angles ranging from 11 degrees to 8.5 degrees. Most of the drivers made in the last five years have adjustable heads with their own screwdrivers. My policy now is not to adjust them from the factory setting as logic tells me that any adjustments are probably an attempt to compensate for my bad swing mechanics. I feel that if I hit the ball with proper technique, I wouldn't need to make club setting adjustments, so now I don't. The purchase of a new driver is always coupled by a great round with a driver that has been rented or borrowed. In 2012, I ordered a Rocket balls driver on Amazon immediately after a terrific round at Druids Glen Golf Club outside of Dublin, Ireland. I tried to buy the actual club I had used from the Druids Glen professional but he refused to sell it to me. In 2005, I was able to persuade the professional at Troon North in Arizona and bought the Ping driver I had rented. In 2002, I bought a new Taylor R-5 driver after another great round at the resort course at Disney World in Florida. Most of these drivers will collect dust or reside in a professional leather bag that sits in my family room in Pebble Beach, California. I never travel with golf clubs unless I'm going to Bandon Dunes or Augusta National, so

I'm constantly using new equipment. The purchase of the Titleist 910-D was particularly outrageous, since I played with a women's version of the club. I bought a complete set of new Titleist clubs for my daughter Meredith, and played with it while playing with her. The Titleist 910-D has survived the Pebble Beach bag and is now the driver of choice for my set of clubs that I keep in Los Angeles.

In the summer of 2012, I visited Brian in England where I have a set of Titleist blades (circa 1990) with steel shafts. The driver in that bag is the first version of the Calloway Big Bertha driver, which I'm no longer comfortable with, so I use Brian's driver which is an older Titleist model with a graphite shaft that seems perfect for me. I corrected this situation when Brian visited us in 2013 (he always travels with his clubs) as I gave him one of my Ping drivers and Ping 3 wood to take back with him and put it in the UK bag which resides at his home.

When I played the round in Ireland at Druids Glen, it was kind of a business event with our attorneys, who are all good players. It seems that everyone in Ireland is a good golfer. I rented a set of Taylor Made clubs, including the Rocketballs driver. I was a little intimidated since we had no warm-up as we proceeded to the first tee. I had never hit the Rocketballs driver, so I chickened out and hit a 3 wood down the middle of the fairway to gain some confidence and feel for the clubs. On the 3rd hole, I took out the Rocketballs driver and laced one straight, true, and long and got pretty excited. This experience continued throughout the day as I striped every driver on a course that is long from the back tees and difficult. I shot 77 that day and was on Cloud 9. I asked the professional if I could buy the driver on the spot and he wouldn't sell it to me because he would have to buy another one to replace it into the rental set. What did I do? I got on my iPad, logged in to Amazon and bought the same club used for $230--and it arrived in San Jose before I returned to the US. It was a great deal, since the club would have been 300 Euros (or $375) if I had bought it from the pro. Once again, good round, good driving--another driver purchased. The Ping acquisition was the same story:

I played in a tournament in Arizona with with a Ping rental set-had a great day with the driver-bought the driver from the club professional. Today, the driver is still the weakest club in many bag. I've just gone back to Rocketballs after some great experience with a custom-made driver, which I'll describe next.

Contrast the driver to the putter. I have played with only three putters (not counting rentals) in my entire life and the first one was stolen out of my garage--a McGregor (Jack Nicklaus) beauty in 1975. I have about fifteen putters but I have used only a White Hot Odyssey putter for the past twenty years. The putters in my other sets are Odyssey derivatives. Putting is absolutely the best part of my game (thanks to Brian).

In 2005, I purchased another set of Taylor Made clubs at the Kingdom at their headquarters in San Diego, where I was fitted after swing video analysism etc. When it came to buying a new putter, we went to the "putting studio" with my Odyssey and they had me try a new Taylor Made putter. The first step was to analyze my putting stroke and select the best option in a new putter. I was then asked to hit fifteen putts with my own putter for the analysis--the putts were all about 15-20 feet. I drained the first ten putts in a row with my own Odyssey putter, to which the Taylor Made sales representative stated, "I don't think we'll be selling you a new putter." The Odyssey remains in my bag today.

CUSTOM CLUBS

I finally did it. In the never- ending search for distance and accuracy with no specific idea in mind, I ended up buying yet another set of clubs on an impulse. I had just spent the entire week in New York City and flown home on a Friday afternoon. I was exhausted, as this usually happens to me when I'm in New York City. The vibrancy and bounce of the city is exhilarating when you arrive, but the noise and hassle quickly sap your energy and enthusiasm for the place. Walt Hussey, a good friend of mine, wanted to play golf on Saturday and he wanted to pick my brain on issues he was having at this job. I told him that there was no way that I was going to play on Saturday, but I would meet him for lunch at my new club, Boulder Ridge in San Jose, where we could hit some balls. I made a lunch reservation and showed up at the club at 11:00 a.m. on Saturday to hit some balls. The club was hosting a custom club fitter, Nakashima Golf, and we went to the range and met their staff including the owner, John Nakashima. I had never heard of them before, but John Nakashima has been making clubs for professionals and amateurs for quite some time and has a studio in Stockton, California. They took some video of my golf swing and came up with an 11-degree driver and I started hitting some balls. Oh my God! I was striping shots right down the middle one after the other. This is usually what happens when you have new golf clubs in your hand--you become a driving range wizard until you actually have to play with the new clubs and then you spend the next six months getting used to them. I was sucked in and couldn't believe how well I was hitting the ball. I had to have this driver, so fifteen minutes later, I was the owner of this $700 custom-made driver. The club felt like putty in my hands and I just kept hitting it straight and long. Well, of course, you can't stop there; they immediately started introducing the irons to me and one by one...I hit all the irons perfectly. They made some shaft adjustments, but within the next hour, I was the owner of a new set of irons and the guys in their truck were customizing the paint job on the clubs. I said "enough" and proceeded to go to lunch while they prepared the package of clubs. When I returned an hour later, John Nakashima asked me to hit a few hybrid clubs that they worked on while I was at lunch. Oh my God! These hybrid clubs were terrific as I hit ball after ball perfectly with a little draw. I said "YES" and became the owner of a new set of clubs which about four times more expensive than anything I had purchased in my life.

The big test would be the next day when I would actually play with these clubs at San Jose Country Club. I approached the round optimistically and was amazed at the result--I hit the new clubs extremely well (a new experience…no break-in period). I was very pleased and shot 76 that day, which isn't far off how I would usually play, but with the new clubs, I had a very consistent ball striking experience. I don't remember missing a fairway with the driver.

It's been nine months since I've had the clubs and I'm still hitting them very well. I'm actually a little shorter with the driver by a few yards, but very consistent. I don't think I missed a fairway in the first 10 rounds I played with the driver, and I'm hitting irons with far more consistent performance. My handicap index was rising before I purchased these clubs and this purchase stopped the skid. I was so pleased with the irons that I had them make me a 4 iron and few wedges. This experience was a first for me with golf equipment and the nice thing is that Nakashima will always adjust things for me if needed. This was the best equipment experience I've ever had in my golfing career.

Chapter 10
THE CURRENT STATE OF THE GAME OF GOLF

Golf is a sport that is in a current state of decline and may not be able to reverse this trend in the foreseeable future. The game will revert to its status of elitism, beyond the economic reach of a large part of the population. The issues are many, but I believe the most significant are that golf is expensive and beyond the economic reach and priority of many families. The other significant issue is that we now live in an era of social media and instant gratification where recreation includes video games where instant results are expected.

The game is expensive. Many private country clubs are struggling to survive and many have gone bankrupt or have had to take on significant debt obligations. The economic recession of 2007-2008 accelerated this trend. New member initiation fees, coupled with monthly dues and food and beverage minimum fees, finance private clubs. The clubs also add transfer fees based on the initiation fee to take advantage of member turnover. It used to be a large investment to fund the initiation fee and the member's monthly household budget would easily be able to handle the monthly dues and food and beverage minimum fees. The trend now is totally reversed. Here are examples of the fees for those items for three private country clubs in the San Francisco Bay Area.

PRIVATE Club	INITIATION Fee-2000	INITIATION Fee-2014
One	$68,000	$19,500
Two	$110,000	$-0-
Three	$250,000	$150,000

MONTHLY DUES FOR EACH CLUB:

One	$150	$600
Two	$400	$950
Three	$1000	$1400

FOOD AND BEVERAGE MINIMUMS ARE:

One	$150/qtr.	$450/qtr.
Two	$450/qtr	$800/qtr
Three	None	None

These situations represent significant trends and all the cases are different, but it's clear that initiation fees, which generally represent an equity interest in the club for the member, are declining significantly while monthly dues and food and beverage minimums are increasing exponentially. The initiation fees are declining due to the significant decline in demand for membership, particularly for a young family that needs the money for home mortgage payments and other priorities such as health care coverage, etc. The initiation fees continue to decline to try and attract enough members to join the club and pay the monthly fees, which are required to maintain the club. The costs of maintaining the club have risen drastically in the past ten years for labor, medical and benefit costs, insurance, and the costs required for the condition of the golf course. The monthly dues used to be an incidental item for the private golf club member and today they are almost equivalent to a home mortgage payment. People will think twice before taking on this type of obligation, irrespective of their income. There isn't much the private country club can do to stem the tide other than to have more tournaments, weddings, and social occasions to use the facilities more efficiently. The economics are simple: there simply isn't enough demand for the product, and the cost-- coupled with the other aspects of golf-- is making the situation difficult for the game. I don't believe the costs of equipment, golf balls, etc. is a big deal, but those prices have also risen significantly over the past ten years. The golf industry has had to resort to continuous equipment design changes (i.e. electronic devices) and new types of golf balls to survive, and the industry is far from a robust investment opportunity.

The other factors contributing to the decline of golf are the time it takes to play a round of golf, the inherent difficulty of the game itself, and the game's inability to attract the game as a family activity. Commitment to a round of golf at a public facility is usually an entire day's affair when you consider transportation time, practice, meals, and the round itself. Most young families will not devote an entire day of the weekend to play golf, especially for those with young children. Today families flock to their youth sports activities and transit kids from one activity to the next, leaving the parent with no time for golf. These recent trends are pretty ingrained in our society and aren't going to change any time soon.

I believe it's important for the USGA to recognize these trends and continue to make the necessary changes and improvements to maintain the character and integrity of the game. I certainly don't have the answers to these questions, but I do have some recommendations. I think the first thing is to "bifurcate" the game to a number of levels where the beginner learns the game properly and is able to play an easy golf course actually designed for the beginner where instruction and practice facilities are readily available. I would advocate the proliferation of 9 hole courses with par 3's, short par 4's, and maybe 1 par 5 in order to give the beginner the opportunity to gain confidence in playing the game. For the current high handicapper who wants to play 18 holes, the courses should be shortened to 5800 to 6000 yards, which will improve the capability of the player and make the rounds more enjoyable. Another alternative is to add shorter tee boxes to existing courses to make the courses easier to play and where the time and pace of play can be improved.

The game of golf is difficult and requires patience, persistence, and a lifetime of learning. Most of us can't play like professionals and never will be able to. Yet golf courses and instruction are geared to trying to emulate the professional, which is impossible to accomplish. Only recently, Jack Nicklaus and Arnold Palmer have started to extol and idea of playing fewer than 18 holes, such as a 13-hole course, and playing from forward or shorter tees to make the game easier and more enjoyable to play.

Youth programs to develop young players aren't sufficient to reverse the current trends of the game. The First Tee program is an outstanding program that develops young players in the right way in instruction and etiquette, and provides an economic opportunity for young people to participate. The First Tee not only produces good golfers, but develops terrific young people.

The last significant factor for the decline of the current game is the absence of "star power" from the professional PGA tour.

The decline of Tiger Woods over the past few years has really hurt the game's ability to attract new people to watch the professionals play.

The emergence of new participative sports (new for the United States) such as cycling, soccer, and walking are putting additional pressure on golf and eating into market share.

I really don't see the reversal of these trends in my lifetime but the First Tee, 13-hole courses, and improvement in instruction are all potential factors that can reduce the pace of the decline.

ACHIEVEMENTS

Golf is mostly a game of failure, so it's not a bad thing to count your blessings and smell the flowers. If you ask the PGA touring professional, they will tell you that they hit probably five shots a round (or less) that they consider acceptable. Every other effort involves some degree of failure, miscalculation, or downright disaster.

If you ask the PGA touring professional about his goals and objectives, the most common answer will be "I just want to get better." In a sense, golf is a bit like baseball where the excellent player makes an out 70% of the time; in golf, failure occurs almost 95% of the time.

One of the things I've always noticed in any of the private country clubs that I have visited all over the world is that when you look at the chronological list of winners of the club championship—it's almost the same guy or gal that wins all the time during the height of their career and then the torch passes to the next dominant player in the club who proceeds on the same path. I can't account for this, as it is almost universal in my experience.

Curtis Strange won two US Opens in a row and he came close to winning three in a row. He was at the height of his powers and then after finishing a close second, he decided he had to get better by hitting the ball longer, and he never contended for the championship again... or much of anything else. It's happened to a number of professionals, such as David Duval, who went from the No. 1 player in the worth to mediocrity. It's just a very tough game. You can plot the game as a pyramid for competition with each leg of the pyramid requiring an exponential improvement in skill.

Chapter 11
PYRAMID OF
COMPETITIVENESS

PGA Tour
PGA Tour-Minor League
PGA Professional Competitions
National USGA Competitions
State USGA Competitions
Tournament Competition-Amateur
Gambling
Weekend Nassau
Casual Round of Golf

The level of skill required to move up the ladder and be successful is an exponential step requiring mental toughness and not necessarily physical skills. The casual round of golf is one that is not competitive and its purpose is mostly social. The casual round of golf is extremely important to the health of the game of golf itself, since most of the rounds played are casual rounds. The casual forms the basis of many friendships and collaborations and may be viewed as a foundation to the rest of the game. Participation is critical to the health of the game and casual rounds spark the interest that make the game interesting, challenging, and fun.

The gap between the professional and the outstanding amateur was never illustrated more vividly than at the 2015 British Open at the Old Course at Saint Andrews. Paul Dunne, an Irish amateur, who played his collegiate golf at the University of Alabama-Birmingham, found himself tied for the lead after the third round of the Open Championship. He had been able to emerge from the pack in obscurity as the rain, wind, and endless delays plagued the tournament to move it to a Monday finish. The media had an entire day to dissect Paul with full page articles about him in the London *Guardian* and the *New York Times*. He could become the first amateur to win the tournament since Bobby Jones in 1930. The attention and publicity afforded Paul was historic and way beyond any of his previous experiences playing golf at the NCAA collegiate level. I'm sure it was a very difficult evening for Paul. The media tracked him to the driving range, as he would be playing in the last group with Louie Oosthuizen. His face on the driving range seemed ashen as he was trying to focus and take it all in. Graham McDowell, the Irish professional, came up to him on the range and seemed to try to coach him. He did not seem relaxed at all and the media attention was making it worse. The round started unceremoniously. The first hole is the easiest driving hole on the course, and he hit an indifferent iron to the 140-yard mark on the left side of the fairway. His approach shot, which needed to carry the Swilcan Burn, was indifferent and fell short of the burn, which was probably the first shot in the entire field for the entire tournament that didn't carry the burn. He was left with a delicate pitch and putt which he failed to execute and started with a bogey.

On the second hole, he hit his drive so far to the right that he had to hit a provisional ball. He hit the provisional ball in the gorse on the right side of the fairway. He then hit a second provisional ball onto the fairway. His first ball was recovered on the practice putting green and he was given a drop and made another bogey. He was clearly a "wreck" and tried to compose himself and actually went out in even par for the front nine. However, the front nine is where all the birdies are, and he shot 42 on the way in for a 78 and 30th place at 6 under par. While at the beginning of the day, he seemed a lock for the low amateur Silver Medal as he was contending for the outright title. He ended up losing the medal as well, as he was bested by two other amateurs. He went from the talk of the sporting world on Sunday to a mere footnote at the close of the tournament on Monday. He is a fine player, but this experience really illustrates the difference that the professional experiences in four days of competition at the highest level in golf.

PERSONAL ACHIEVEMENTS

My golf career has been unremarkable and undistinguished. I've won a few low gross score tournaments, a Senior Pro-Am event with Jim Colbert, and some minor club events. My handicap over the past ten years has ranged from 1.1 to 7 and is currently 3.6. I am disappointed that I can't execute that handicap in competition, so I'm going back to the drawing board with a PGA professional in tow to try and figure out why I can't play to my handicap in competition. If I can't compete at my handicap level, I can't figure out why I seem to play very well immediately after a competitive event. I know I need more length off the tee, and that's what I hope the lessons will accomplish. I also need to be more consistent so I can routinely depend on my ability to execute under some pressure. I suspect this is the case at every level in the golf pyramid.

If you talk to golfers, most of the talk focuses on the negative--the things that they are not good at, rather than what their abilities. I always advise them to remember the good shots and treat the bad shots as excursions. We all want to get better at a game where perfection is impossible.

Losing all the negativity for the moment, I'm now going to chronicle my most significant achievements in golf.

I have four hole-in-ones. Three of those hole-in-ones have occurred on the same hole--the 18th hole at Pasatiempo--and the fourth one is on the second hole of Cordevalle Golf Club.

The 18th hole at Pasatiempo is a treacherous par 3 where you have to carry your tee shot over a gorge with bunkers surrounding the greens on all sides. The green slopes severely from back to front and slides toward the gorge. The slope of the green from back to front is getting worse as erosion and ground settlement have set in over the years. In the remodel of the course in 2008, the hole became even more sloped and a collection area of grass now sits at the foot of the hole below the green. When the green is dry, a shot hit at the hole will roll off the green and end up in the collection area.

My first hole-in-one on 18 was from the championship tee of 187 yards in 2001 with a 7 wood that hit the green and bounced in the hole on one hop. The tees were reconfigured in 2007, so this tee no longer exists. The championship tee is now at 170 yards. Ironically, my second hole-in-one was from 152 yards on a tee that was the championship tee for that particular day but had moved up due to maintenance. This tee no longer exists either. Since the remodel in 2007, I thought it would be impossible to make a hole-in-one there due to severe slope and speed of the green. Many shots were ending up in the collection area in the front of the green just over the gorge despite the fact that the ball could land 5-10 feet from the hole. In December, 2012, we were finishing a three-ball match. We had started at 7:00 a.m. and therefore there was a bit of moisture on the green. In Northern California, particularly in coastal areas, morning dew and fog are prevalent before burning off to bright sunshine in mid-day. It was about 10:30 a.m. as we approached the 18th. I decided to hit a seven iron from the tees we were playing that day at 143 yards. You now have to hit the ball past the hole to have any chance of getting it close and stopping. I hit it perfectly and it landed about 15-18 past the hole. Due to the slope of the hole, the ball started rolling toward the pin. I thought it was a nice shot and I would have a decent opportunity for birdie. After a few seconds, the ball started rolling toward the hole slowly and it got closer and closer and we all got excited. I was amazed, with my mouth wide open, and after a few more seconds, it rolled some more, hit the flagstick, and went in. I really couldn't believe it.

I also have 16 eagle 2's on par 4 holes including 2 on one hole-the 11th at Spanish Bay Golf Links at Pebble Beach. I also have one of the difficult 17th hole at Spanish Bay. On foreign soil, I made an eagle 2 at the second hole at Portmarnock in Ireland.

CONCLUSION

Golf has been wonderful for my life, since I continuously require a challenge and can never accept the status quo. I grew up in the inner city in New Haven, Connecticut and spent my youth playing baseball, basketball and football. Golf was for sissies and, something that was far beyond my middle-class economic status.

As I discovered the age of twenty-five, golf provided all the challenge I could ever want, as I found the game to be quite difficult. One in a while, you would hit a perfect shot, which offset all the poor play you had experienced. I've been fortunate to be able to play some of the greatest courses in the world and have now played 85 of the top 100 courses in the United States. I've played every British Open venue in England and Scotland at least twice.

I've met some wonderful people through the years on the golf course who have provided many different perspectives on life. The game enabled me to focus on trying to continuously improve my technique, providing significant stress relief from the daily machinations of a business career. Golf enabled me to spend time with my son from age six to the present day and when you play golf with your son, you always win...you win if you beat him, and you win if he beats you and goes home and brags to this mother. There is nothing more satisfying for me than to play with him.

I'll keep playing until I'm no longer physically able, and I hope that's a long way into the future.

READ THE FOLLOWING WITH CAUTION

THE "SHANKS"

What are "the Shanks?" The Shank is equivalent to the un-
speakable four-letter word. It is a word that goes unspoken in the
world of golf. You would not wish "the Shank" on your worst enemy in the world. It is a vile term that evokes fear and trepidation
in the psyche of every golfer who has played the game including
the professional. It is equivalent to a bad case of chicken pox or
measles and if not eradicated causes anxiety, depression, embarrassment, hopelessness and incredible misery to a golfer. When
we think of how many times a day, we hear the constant barrage
of four letter words from the populace, the word "shank" is never
uttered on the golf course. The possibility of a shank is grounds
for termination from participation. It not only affects the player,
the shank impacts the psyche, routine, and technique of any participant that even observes the "shank."

So, what is a shank or what are the "Shanks." I went to the
dictionary shuttering to even look up the word. In golf, it is defined as "to hit a golf ball with the base of the shaft of a club
just above the club head causing the ball to go off sharply to the
right." This definition is the most benign designation for the shank
that I could ever think of.

While there are cures for the Shank, there are no symptoms. The Shank merely appears as if an angry god or even God itself is extracting punishment. The Shank appears and grips the player into total fear taking hold of its victim and shaking the player to the foundation of every thing ever learned about the game of golf. The Shank repeats and grabs its victim and terror and potential carnage can result.

Some examples:

- If you have seen the movie, "Tin Cup", driving range professional, Roy McAvoy (played by Kevin Costner) qualifies for the US Open. It is an improbable march through the qualifying events, and McAvoy anxiously practices and gets ready for the experience of his career. On the eve of when he supposed to leave for the event, he is on the range and "The Shanks" appear from nowhere after he has made hundreds of good swings. Balls wildly bounce to the right a few yards off the teeing area and terror strikes. His swing is gone, he keeps "shanking, " smashing objects to the right and the sounds of clinking from the shaft and clanging from the objects he's hitting are deafening. He has no idea of what to do or how to correct the situation, which is exactly what happens with "the Shanks." He then heads for the US Open venue. On the practice range with all the other professionals warming up, McAvoy continues to shank. He is moments away from having to tee it up at the US Open and the shanks are still present as he dribbles a few balls over the toes of Phil Mickelson on the range.

- A real life experience occurred when Brian and I entered a tournament at our club. The tournament was a three-day event and the highlight event on the calendar of the club. Wednesday was the practice round and Brian was playing very well and I was encouraged that we might do well in the event. On Thursday morning, we had a 9:00 AM starting time, so we went to the range for a normal warm-up. Out of nowhere, Brian hit his first shot and it went sailing over the fence into the eleventh fairway at a 90 degree angle about 30 yards off the tee. Oh my God! I couldn't believe it. Brian has "the Shanks" and we tee off in less than an hour! He was a mess. The more he tried, the worse it became. I had to do something or we wouldn't be able to play at all. I went running in to the clubhouse and ran up to the teaching professional and exclaimed, "Brian has a case of "the Shanks!" You have to help him and you have to help him NOOOWWW! The professional winked and proceeded to the range to provide the required assistance. Brian was distraught and crest fallen but the professional straightened him out quickly with a few minor changes and off we went. The Shanks come from some very dark place in the golfing universe and no one quite knows how they come and how they go away.

- Another terrible experience was a round at Stanwich Golf Club in Greenwich, Connecticut. Stanwich is a wonderful venue and this a special treat for me. Our foursome walked to the first hole to commence play. About 10 yards to the right of the first tee, a worker was attending to a flowerbed weeding and fertilizing the arrangements by the tee. Three of us hit away and the fourth player proceeded to tee it up. He was clearly the weakest member of the group, but we didn't care as we were looking forward to a great day. As he began his swing, I began to wince and become concerned. My concerns were validated. The ball went whizzing by the worker's head and just missed him no more than 10 yards to the right of the first tee. It could have been a disaster but again-it was "The Shanks." Fortunately for him, and us it didn't happen again and no one could figure out how it happened in the first place.

"The Shanks" can happen to great players as well. One morning, one of our best players in the club teed the ball up on the first hole. He is a scratch handicap player with great length off the tee. He approaches the first tee shot, swings and smacks the ball from the first tee to the roof of the clubhouse on the ninth green, which is perpendicular to the first tee. The ball traveled about 20 yards on a right angle. Incredible! It was the only shot he would miss on that day.

"The Shanks" is the worst thing that can happen to any golfer, a shot off the hosel of the club that produces nothing but misery and heartache. It is such a vile occurrence that I could not place it in the body of this book. It is placed here to remind us of its existence as a part of golf that is not to be experienced.

CPSIA information can be obtained
at www.ICGtesting.com
Printed in the USA
BVOW06*0819080317
478093BV00003B/5/P